The Future of Criminal Justice

The Future of Criminal Justice

Resettlement, chaplaincy and community

Edited by

Christopher Jones and
Peter Sedgwick

Published in Great Britain in 2002 by
Society for Promoting Christian Knowledge
Holy Trinity Church
Marylebone Road
London NW1 4DU

British Library Cataloguing-in-Publication Data
A catalogue record for this book is available from the British Library

ISBN 0-281-05483-5

10 9 8 7 6 5 4 3 2 1

Designed and typeset by Kenneth Burnley, Wirral, Cheshire.
Printed in Great Britain by Antony Rowe Ltd, Chippenham, Wiltshire.

Contents

About the Contributors

Paul Cavadino is Chief Executive at Nacro, where he has worked since 1972. He was Chair of the Penal Affairs Consortium from 1989 to 2001, and Clerk to the Parliamentary All-Party Penal Affairs Group from 1980 to 2001.

Jane Clay describes herself as a cockney, brought up on a large council estate in Dagenham. She trained as a teacher in Sheffield and worked part-time in HMP Wakefield before becoming one of the Chaplains in 1996 at HMP New Hall (a women's prison near Wakefield). She is an Honorary Canon of Wakefield Cathedral.

David Faulkner CB is Chair of the Howard League, Secretary of the Centre for Criminological Research at Oxford University, and formerly Deputy Secretary, Home Office.

Julia Flack is a probation officer in Cambridgeshire and was a member of General Synod from 1985 to 1998. She was also a member of the Board for Social Responsibility and its Home Affairs Committee and now chairs the Criminal Justice Committee in Ely Diocese.

Myra Fulford is Director of PACT (Prison Advice & Care Trust) which was created from a merger of a number of charities in 2001. She was previously Director of the Bourne Trust from 1998 to 2001 (until its merger with PACT), and Director of the Manic Depression Fellowship from 1992 to 1998.

John Harding CBE is a Visiting Professor in Criminal Justice Studies at the University of Hertfordshire, and a member of the Parole Board for

England and Wales. He was the Chief Probation Officer of the Inner London Probation Service until April 2001. He was also a member of the Anglican Board for Social Responsibility (BSR) Home Affairs Committee from 1996 to 2001.

Christopher Jones is Chaplain and Fellow of St Peter's College, Oxford. He has previously served as Chaplain to a Remand Centre and from 1995 to 2001 was a member of the Prison Chaplaincy Advisory Group.

Baroness Helena Kennedy practises predominantly in criminal law. She has acted in many leading British cases including the Brighton Bombing Trial and Guildford Four Appeal. She is Chair of the British Council, Chair of the Human Genetics Commission and is on the Advisory Council of the World Bank Institute. She has been a Life Peer since 1997 and is a Bencher of Gray's Inn. She is a Member of the Académie Universelle des Cultures, a Fellow of the Royal Society of Arts, a Fellow of the City and Guilds Institute and the Chair of the London International Festival of Theatre.

May El Komy has worked for Nacro for six months and is a Research & Policy Officer at their Race and Criminal Justice Unit. She has a BA in Law and Criminology and an MA in International Criminology.

Juliet Lyon is the Director of the Prison Reform Trust. Previously she worked in applied psychology, education and mental health. She is a professional adviser to Childline and recently worked on the reference groups for the review of the sentencing framework and the Social Exclusion Unit's review of preventing re-offending.

Tim Newell worked as a prison governor for 37 years, retiring in 2002 after ten years as governor of Grendon Underwood Prison, the therapeutic community for dangerous and damaged prisoners. He gave the 2000 Swarthmore lecture for the Religious Society of Friends published as *Forgiving Justice*. He is currently involved in developing restorative practices in custodial and resettlement settings with the Prison Service and with the Quakers. He was also a member of the BSR Home Affairs committee.

William Noblett was appointed Chaplain General and Archdeacon to HM Prisons in July 2001. Prior to this, he was one of the Prison Service's most experienced and respected Chaplains, serving at Wakefield (where he began his prison ministry in 1987), Norwich and Full Sutton Prison in Yorkshire. He is a Canon of York Minster.

General Sir David Ramsbotham was commissioned into the Rifle Brigade, later the Royal Green Jackets, in 1958, after National Service and obtaining a History degree at Corpus Christi College, Cambridge. He retired from the Regular Army in 1993, as Adjutant General and an ADC (General) to HM The Queen. He was Her Majesty's Chief Inspector of Prisons from December 1995 to July 2001.

Peter Sedgwick has been Assistant Secretary, Board for Social Responsibility since 1996 and is the Church of England's policy officer on drugs, alcohol, mental health and criminal justice. He was previously a lecturer in theology at Hull University (1988 to 1994) and a Fulbright Fellow at the Center for Theological Inquiry, Princeton, New Jersey in 1991.

Lord Woolf became Lord Chief Justice in 2000. He was previously a Lord Justice of Appeal from 1986 to 1992, a Lord of Appeal in Ordinary from 1992 to 1996, and was Master of the Rolls from 1996 to 2000. He held an inquiry into prison disturbances ('The Woolf Report') in 1990 and into Access to Justice between 1994 and 1996. He was made a Life Peer in 1992.

Dedicated to

the Right Reverend Robert Hardy,
Bishop to Prisons 1985–2001

Foreword

LAST YEAR A HUGE CONGREGATION gathered in Lincoln Cathedral to say farewell to their retiring bishop, Robert Hardy. Some of us were there in particular to bear witness to his work as Bishop to Prisons for 16 years. This book is moved by the same feeling of gratitude.

But Bob Hardy has always been a man to look forward, not back, and any book in his honour must do the same.

Our criminal justice system is a field containing plenty of good and bad elements – the wheat and the tares grow thickly together. There are many different labourers in the field, each with their own tools – academics, judges, prison officers, chaplains, voluntary workers – and therefore their own point of view. Our media are afraid of complexity and tend to oversimplify each aspect of criminal justice without recognizing the links between them. This makes it hard for government ministers and Parliament to continue on a consistent line of policy long enough to achieve results.

This book of essays by practitioners in different parts of the field is therefore of great help. It draws together in readable form the lessons which they have gained from their own experience. It will help to form that fuller public understanding of how the system works and what is wrong with it which is an essential background for successful reform.

THE RT HON LORD HURD OF WESTWELL CH CBE PC

Introduction

THE PURPOSE OF THIS BOOK on the criminal justice system can be simply stated. There are many people involved with the criminal justice system. Some are professionals, some volunteers, some victims and some offenders. It is not clear to many people what the purpose of the whole system is. It could be replied that the system needs no justification: it just is, in the same way as teaching or health exists in its own right. The danger with such an argument is that the system takes over in its own right: like a juggernaut, it rolls on regardless.

The criminal justice system is undergoing great change, and the successful outcome of this change depends on whether it achieves a coherence that can be respected. One of the contributions from a faith-based perspective is that it can help the voluntary and statutory sectors work together. That will enable some sort of coherence, and it is one which the prison service takes very seriously at this time. Beyond that there is the vexed question, 'What is the purpose of criminal justice in England at this time?' That is not an easy question to answer, for the claims of tabloid journalism and moral unease at the results of a huge rise in unemployment over the last decade seemed in the public perception to be causing a crime wave. The reality was that crime figures began to fall in the 1990s, but for many people the perception was very different. This obscured any vision of how a criminal justice system could deliver a just and workable solution to the needs of society, offender and victim alike.

All the contributors have played their part in trying to answer that question in the last decade. Some have been well known, while others have worked in prisons, probation and voluntary charities. The book begins with four essays which spell out the foundations of a just criminal justice system. One is a philosophical reflection by David Faulkner, who has addressed these issues over many years, most recently in his book *Crime, State and Punishment*. Another gives a theological answer, and is written by Christopher Jones. Between these two essays is one on the political foundation for reform (Juliet Lyon) and one on jurisprudence (Helena Kennedy). We then go to an extended consideration of prisons and prisoners. The Lord Chief Justice asks what constructive role prisons can have, and his ideas are taken up by Sir David Ramsbotham, who was until last year Chief Inspector of Prisons. Jane Clay, who is chaplain in a women's prison, and William Noblett, the Chaplain General, look at the beliefs and values of prisoners, and how chaplaincy can serve the needs of prisoners. Finally Myra Fulford, who has worked in the charities world for many years, offers an interesting perspective on the prisoner as volunteer.

We then turn to a series of essays on the criminal justice system as a whole. John Harding, as a member of the Parole Board, and formerly Chief Probation Officer for Inner London, writes about the risks in releasing a person from custody. Paul Cavadino, Director of Nacro, and May El Komy, also from Nacro, describe the results of their surveys of racism in the criminal justice system. Tim Newell, who was until recently Governor of Grendon Underwood Prison, then describes his vision of restorative justice. Finally we return to the place of the Church, with two articles. Julia Flack was for many years a member of General Synod, as well as working as a probation officer, and she asks what role congregations can have in working for change in the criminal justice system. The other essay is a reflection on a person who inspired many of the contributors to this book. Bishop Bob Hardy was Bishop to Prisons from 1985 to 2001, as well as being Bishop of Maidstone from 1980 to 1987 and then Bishop of Lincoln from 1987 to 2001. The book is dedicated, with great respect and affection, to him. The essay shows how a Bishop can still give leadership in this area, even in as pluralist a society as England is today.

The future of criminal justice will depend on a coherent answer being given to all these issues. Those who work within the system, or who comment on it, know all too well the paradox of ever greater change, government reviews and initiatives, while the stubborn reality of an overcrowded system remains in place. There have been improvements over the last decade, many of them due to the work of the contributors to this book. This collection of essays provides a glimpse into a world that is often not discussed with the depth and seriousness that it deserves. Prisoners and offenders need to be treated as full members of our society, and not relegated to the edges. That is the conviction which motivates all those who write here.

Finally I should like to thank three people: Ana Barrandalla Agona, my secretary, for her skill in working on the manuscript; Christopher Jones, my co-editor; and Ruth McCurry, from SPCK. Without them, this book would not have been possible.

PETER SEDGWICK
December 2002

1 | Principles, Structures and a Sense of Direction

David Faulkner

THIS CHAPTER looks at what is happening in criminal justice and in public service, and in British society more generally; it considers the opportunities and dangers which the present situation presents, and asks what needs to be done; and finally and more tentatively it reflects on what it all means for Christians, or for the liberal or professional conscience.

What is happening in criminal justice

Crime and criminal justice have become much more politicized over the last 20 years. Not much divides the political parties on issues of substance (it never has), but the style of argument has become increasingly adversarial and confrontational. More issues are treated as matters of political rather than professional judgement. Governments must have the solution to everything and always seem to be in charge. There is plenty to criticize and put right, but they have seemed almost to enjoy presenting public servants as 'failing' so that they can take credit for programmes of modernization and reform.

Politics demands slogans – a war on crime or on drugs, zero tolerance, prison works, no more excuses; and instant solutions – night courts, on-the-spot fines, the creation of even more criminal offences. Once examined, the slogans have no real content and the solutions often turn out to be unworkable. 'Liberal' has become a term of abuse, and even those who still hold passionately to the liberal principles of equity, due process, respect for individuals and personal freedom have difficulty in coming to terms with terrorism, racial or religious violence and the more appalling crimes of murder, especially those against children.

There is a strong belief in management and efficiency; in central direction; in uniformity and standardization; in the discipline of targets, performance indicators and financial incentives; and in the ability of those measures to 'drive up standards' and 'deliver results'. That discipline is often salutary, but it can also result in a loss of trust and a culture of blame. There is ample evidence of the way in which a regime of targets and indicators has had perverse effects in the health service and on the railways; Peter Neyroud and Alan Beckley have shown how it can also affect policing and police integrity (Neyroud and Beckley 2001).

There is an accompanying belief in technology – information technology, DNA testing, CCTV – and its ability to produce new and dramatic solutions, reminiscent of the 'white heat of technological revolution' in the 1960s. Of course technology should be developed and exploited, but the solutions are only as good as the services' professional judgement about how it can and should be used, and their skill in using it. New techniques of risk assessment are a useful guide in anticipating and managing risks to individuals or to the public, but they are still for the most part uncertain in their reliability and have the potential for serious injustice if they are misused. The government is rightly committed to the monitoring and evaluation of its new and existing policies and to building them on the principle of 'what works', and it has promoted a massive and thoroughly welcome programme of evaluative research. But it has still shown some ambivalence when the results turn out to be politically inconvenient, for example over the effectiveness of sentencing in deterring crime.

There is still in government, and in the country as a whole, an implicit belief in the existence of a 'criminal class' who are somehow different from 'people like us'. They may be thought of as being capable of being 'rescued' or 'reformed', or more often simply deterred, by the effect of government policies; but otherwise they need to be controlled by the criminal justice process, or ultimately put out of action through sentences of imprisonment. The criminal law, the police and the criminal justice process are seen as capable of preventing crime and controlling those who commit it without much help from the rest of society. If they are not succeeding, it is the fault of the system and those who work in it, not of any unrealistic expectations of what it can actually achieve. It is not 'our' responsibility.

Other influences have come from a different direction. The European Convention on Human Rights began to influence penal policy in the 1970s, and the processes of government have been subject to the discipline of judicial review from about the same time. Although government and the courts are still working out the full implications of the Convention's incorporation into the Human Rights Act 1998, and are often ambivalent in their attitude towards it, the Act should still mark a turning point. Human rights, and the collective and individual responsibilities which go with them, should now be taken seriously in every area of public policy and professional practice.

Influenced by the report of the Stephen Lawrence inquiry (Macpherson 1999) and the report of the Commission on the Future of Multi-Ethnic Britain (2000), the country is beginning to realize that a modern society has not only to prevent racial discrimination, but actively to promote racial equality and to value and celebrate diversity. Some people still feel genuinely, if misguidedly, threatened by the presence of minority groups, and both reports were stridently and sometimes dishonestly criticized. But the debate seems on the whole to be becoming more rational and open-minded, and arguments can less easily be dismissed for being 'politically correct'. Differences in religion add a new dimension to the argument, especially after the terrorist attacks in the United States on 11 September 2001.

Developments in policy and practice

At a more practical level, there is an increasing emphasis on the prevention of crime through local, community-based partnerships involving the statutory, voluntary and community sectors. Those partnerships are often linked to social policies such as Sure Start and the Connexions Service which aim to reduce the disadvantage, poverty and social exclusion that are associated with criminality. Victims of crime are for the most part receiving more recognition and respect, although there is more still to be done, and attempts to give them more of a 'voice' should stop short of opportunities for them to demand a particular sentence or to exploit them for the benefit of the offender or the system. Just as the prevention of crime is a civic responsibility for citizens and communities as a whole, and not just a matter for criminal justice, so is recognition and support for victims.

The most challenging set of contemporary ideas is that associated with relational and restorative justice. Relational justice is one of several themes which are being pursued by the Relationships Foundation in Cambridge. It is described in the Foundation's book on relational justice (Burnside and Baker 1994) and there are regular reports in the *Relational Justice Bulletin.* Restorative justice is a more narrow concept and is typically thought of as a procedure which brings the offender and the victim, often with their families, together in a restorative conference leading to some form of negotiated settlement or restitution. The procedure can, however, take different forms, not all of them necessarily involving the individual victim, and it can take effect at various stages of the criminal justice process or as an alternative to criminal proceedings altogether. The idea is formalized in the referral orders which courts have, since April 2002, been required to make on juvenile offenders appearing before them for the first time, unless they are discharged or sentenced to custody. Restorative justice is usually associated with young offenders and less serious offences, but it is also being explored, for example, as a way of resolving conflicts in prisons.

It is at present unclear whether restorative justice will remain at the margins of the criminal justice process, or enter the main stream; whether it will displace the traditional adversarial process, or become integrated within it; or whether it will introduce a new set of relationships and dynamics, or become in the end little more than a new vocabulary to describe and justify existing practices. Martin Wright and Tim Newell are amongst those who have described how the idea might be applied and the results it might achieve (Wright 1999; Newell 2000).

So far as the government is concerned, the policy debate was at the time of writing (early 2002) focused mainly on the reviews of sentencing (Halliday 2001) and of the criminal courts (Auld 2001), and reform of the police (Home Office 2001). That debate was for a time overshadowed by the passage of the Anti-Terrorism, Crime and Security Act, whose provision on detention without trial, religious hatred and the application of European standards revealed a deeper and more polarized division of opinion, especially in the House of Lords, than had been seen for some time. It was too early, at the time of writing, to predict whether those divisions would continue and spread to other areas of debate, whether they would recede with the passage of time, or what the outcome of the reviews of sentencing and the criminal courts might be.

Conflict and integrity

Whatever the outcome, the underlying issues about the nature of justice, the ethical base for professional practice, the purpose of punishment, the rights and responsibilities of citizenship, and the accountability and legitimacy of criminal justice and other public services will continue to be of fundamental importance and to demand principled and rigorous debate.

It is not the purpose of this chapter to take sides in an argument about which elements in this situation deserve approval and which deserve criticism. There is much to applaud, and much that gives cause for concern. In most matters of legislation and policy, the outcome depends as much on the way in which those on the ground put them into practice as they do on the legislation and policy themselves. Much recent legislation gives powers to the police and creates criminal offences which the police can use or enforce at their discretion, for example over harassment, public order and terrorism. Most of the issues involve resolving conflicts. Some conflicts will be ethical – for example between public protection and respect for the individual, or between equality and diversity. Some will be professional – perhaps between speed and the need for consultation, or between economy and accountability. Some will be managerial – to meet different targets or satisfy different budgetary requirements. Risks must be managed and not simply avoided. Families or victims may need to be involved. Local interests may be different from those of central government, or they may themselves conflict with one another. There may be commercial interests to take into account, including those of shareholders where the private sector is involved. Considerations of race, ethnicity or religion will often be present. And there will always be pressure to show results, and increasingly to do so in terms of centrally imposed targets and indicators and with fewer resources.

How the conflicts are resolved will largely depend on the personal and professional values of public servants and the framework of accountability within which they operate. It will depend on their integrity and working culture, their professional wisdom, their sense of confidence and trust, and the extent to which they have discretion to apply their own judgement. Their working situation has inevitably and rightly become more rigorous and demanding over the past 20 years. But it has also become more complex and more ambiguous. The 'performance culture' of effectiveness and 'what works' is sometimes represented as if it were 'value free', and as if ethical considerations need not arise. Individuals may be driven by personal ambition and a desire to succeed; but a sense of public service or duty brings few rewards, and conscience becomes a self-indulgence which they cannot afford. Criminal justice is seen as a process leading to an output, such as convictions and sentences, and to outcomes such as public protection, public confidence or the satisfaction of the victim. Justice is not seen as an outcome itself – a resolution of a situation which is as fair as the circumstances permit to all those who may be involved and which has been achieved by due process.

What needs to be done

It is easy to say that criminal justice needs more resources – money, staff, buildings (especially prisons), technology. So it does, and that is not seriously denied, although there is a serious argument about whether too much is being invested in imprisonment and too little in prevention and rehabilitation. But other kinds of resource are just as important – leadership; relationships; the skills and time to listen, consult and motivate; a culture of mutual respect and public duty; and a structure of accountability, not just to central government, but also to citizens and communities. Services, especially those in criminal justice, need to be not only accountable but also legitimate in the sense that they can command authority and respect (Beetham 1991; Sparks *et al.* 1996; Bottoms 2001). Citizens should themselves feel some sense of responsibility for, and take some pride in, the country's criminal justice and other public services – not least its prisons. Parliament, government, the courts, public services, civil society and citizens need to work together in a relationship which is not collusive, élitist or exclusionary, as it may sometimes have been in the past; which is not oppressive or authoritarian; but which is one of accountability, integrity, confidence and trust.

All that may seem very fine and large, and it can still be said that what counts is what people actually experience, what they see and hear, whether they think they are getting value for their money. In criminal justice that includes how far they feel safe and protected. But citizens also expect quality as well as quantity, and those less tangible resources are just as important as money, management and technology.

A programme for reforming public – and especially criminal justice – services might begin by establishing some principles. For example:

- respect for human dignity and for people as citizens and a more developed sense of the rights and responsibilities of citizenship;
- a positive commitment to promoting racial equality and valuing diversity;
- proportionality of response whenever the state or its servants have to intervene in citizens' lives;
- decisions to be taken and services to be provided as locally as practicable;
- openness, transparency and accessibility;
- accountability, taking multiple forms and operating in several directions, both nationally and locally;
- a commitment to human rights and the European Convention on Human Rights, recognizing that the Convention is not just a statement of individual rights but also a framework for personal and collective responsibilities in a civilized, liberal democratic society.

The programme would then apply these principles to the various services and processes. Where necessary it would question the services' organizational structure and professional culture, and the purpose, legitimacy and effectiveness of the various processes. In some important aspects a programme of this kind is already moving forward – the creation of the Youth Justice Board and youth offender teams, the formation of the National Probation Service, the proposals on sentencing and the criminal courts from the Halliday and Auld reports, and the proposed reform of the police. Less prominent but no less significant are the review of the targets and indicators set by the government under the Public Service Agreements which it introduced soon after coming into office; the methods by which services and new initiatives are funded and the bureaucracy and frustrations which are often associated with them; and the next Comprehensive Spending Review (2002).

So too are the developments which are now taking place in the role of the voluntary and community sector, and of civil society more generally, including churches and faith groups. All those developments need to be consciously informed by principles and values of the kind indicated in the previous paragraph.

More specific points of focus, relating to what the government would call cross-cutting issues, would include:

- education and training, not just in skills and competences – although there is a need for that, especially in consultation and risk-taking – but also to provide what Mike Nellis (2001) has called 'overarching' as distinct from 'underpinning' knowledge. In other words, what distinguishes universities from colleges of further education, or leadership from management;
- a change in the balance of power and decision-making from the national to more local level – from centralized, monolithic bureaucracies to more devolved structures which are closer to the citizens they serve;
- a change in the arrangements for funding research and innovative projects to encourage initiative and imagination, to allow more flexibility and more continuity, and to encourage more long-term vision (Hood 2001).

A government with a long-term vision would also want to look at some of the architecture of the state, and to consider for example a Department of Justice, a Supreme Court, a legitimate Second Chamber of Parliament, a commission on human rights, and an independent commission for judicial appointments. It should also consider an institute or college for leadership in the criminal justice services and professions (Faulkner 2001).

This chapter has so far been about how to improve the country's system of justice. It has implicitly argued that the services which make up the criminal justice system share most of the characteristics and problems of public services generally. All of them operate within the fabric of society as a whole. The criminal justice system is obviously concerned with crime, preventing it where possible, punishing it when necessary and repairing the harm if it can. But preventing crime and repairing the harm are also the responsibility of other services, of civil society and of citizens as individuals; and although judicial punishment is the state's business and no one else's, there are always difficult, perhaps insoluble, questions about state punishment – how much, what kind, what for, with what purpose. The legitimacy and integrity of its criminal justice system are a necessary condition and one of the tests of a civilized society, but there are real limitations to what the system can be expected to achieve. For the prevention of crime, for repairing the harm it causes, for restoring the offender and the victim, for reconciliation, atonement and forgiveness, one has to look elsewhere. The country must not look only to criminal justice to deal with the problem of crime, still less problems of social disorder, and it must not create what Thomas Hobbes (1651) called Leviathan and David Garland (2001) called a criminal justice state.

What it means for Christians

So to the last and most tentative part of this chapter – what does it all mean for Christians, and for the liberal or professional conscience? It is not acceptable in a modern democratic state to adopt or resist policies or practices on grounds of religious doctrine alone, and most Christians would accept that an action or form of behaviour may be sinful without it having to be made a criminal offence against the state. Religious belief will penetrate further into people's lives than the state, but so far as the state and its institutions are concerned it should do so as a matter of individual choice and not as a requirement of the criminal law or a condition of citizenship. There may, however, be some practices, arguably approved by some versions of some religions, which are so repugnant to society as a whole that the state should not tolerate them. Those who are liable to suffer from them are then entitled to the state's protection.

A modern democratic state must also, in principle, accord different religions equal respect, both under its law and in the operation and management of its institutions. This is more difficult territory. There are sometimes problems in defining what counts as a religion, and there may be occasions when representatives of a religious faith have to be constrained in what they say and do, especially when acting in that capacity in the state's institutions, for example in prisons. Catholic emancipation is now ancient history (except for the Royal Family), and the special position of the Church of England, not only in the constitution but again for example in prisons, is hard to justify in modern circumstances. But there are arguments for institutionalizing spiritual values in some form, the benefits extend beyond the Church of England and its members, and they are often acknowledged by members of other denominations and other faiths.

Even if it is no longer acceptable to argue for a particular policy or practice on religious grounds alone, Christian ideas can still inform, sometimes inspire and occasionally constrain new developments. *Crime, Justice and the Demands of the Gospel* (Board for Social Responsibility 1991), with a Foreword by Robert Hardy, described the state of criminal justice and penal policy as it was at the beginning of the 1990s, and reviewed the contribution which Christian thinking had made over the 15 or so years before that – the Manchester Consultation in 1978, the work of the British Council of Churches Penal Policy Group, *Faith in the City* (report of the Archbishop of Canterbury's Commission on Urban Priority Areas 1985), the Lincoln Conferences in 1989 and 1991. Robert Hardy had made a powerful contribution to all of these, and convened the Lincoln Conferences. The paper quoted Adrian Speller's seven important points for Christian thinking about penal policy (Speller 1986).

1   The State has a positive task under God to protect the community against crime and aggression for the sake of the common good;

2   There is a basic equality of human beings before God; in discharging the complex problems of responsibility in the penal field, the place of the victim, the offender and the community have all to be considered;

3   The Gospel priority is to serve the poor and those to whose care no prestige is attached;

4   Structures of power always need scrutiny. There is a presumption in favour of participating in decision-making wherever possible, including the treatment of criminals;

5   Punishment as retribution is a basic justification, but it must be based on deserts and it must be distinguished from revenge. Once this is granted there must be a hope of reformation in it, the conditions and possibilities of this being

faced realistically with due consideration for the personal integrity of the criminal;

6 The recognition that not only the offender, but judge, jury, society – everyone – is alike a sinner and at the same time enfolded within God's graciousness, should deepen the sense of delegated responsibility for judgement and for compassion in its exercise;

7 The constant awareness that our penal laws, like our whole network of social sanctions and customs are fallible . . . all our judgements, penal or otherwise, are necessary but defective in the light of the final judgement of God.

The paper drew attention to the muddled state of official and professional thinking about sentencing and penal practice, emphasized the importance of retaining the rehabilitative ideal, and considered the significance of Christian ideas such as punishment, forgiveness, repentance, atonement, penance, mercy, reconciliation and restitution, all of which are as relevant to the present debate as they were ten years ago. It addressed questions of accountability, proportionality, human rights and citizenship, none of which were prominent in official thinking at that time, and looked forward to the development of restorative justice. It concluded:

In conclusion, a strong case exists, both morally and pragmatically, for a criminal justice system which puts a high premium on the value of parental responsibility and citizenship; which properly supports and compensates the victim of crime; which invests time and money on practical crime prevention programmes; which deals with petty offences outside of criminal courts as far as possible; which sees community penalties as normative; which reserves custodial sentences for serious offenders; which treats prisoners with proper respect by acknowledging their basic human rights and encourages their return to the community as full participatory members. Such a criminal justice system may be described as essentially locally based, participative and humane in approach. It is also one which reflects the demands of the Gospel.

The church's ministry to prisons, with which Robert Hardy has for so long been associated, should be a ministry not just to prisoners, and especially not just to prisoners who claim an Anglican allegiance, but to the institution and its community as a whole. There are obvious difficulties when there are multi-faith communities, governors vary in their degree of interest and support, and staff can sometimes be unhelpful or even obstructive. But it is a sad state of affairs if the chaplaincy is seen just as a 'service provider' alongside several others.

It is interesting that there is now discussion of a ministry to the police (Field-Smith 2001), and a similar case could be made for a ministry to the National Probation Service.

A context in which religious belief may be particularly helpful is where a person – for the purpose of this chapter a criminal justice manager or practitioner – is or ought to be troubled as a matter of conscience. It will be rare for a matter of conscience to lead to resignation or 'whistle blowing', though that will sometimes happen. More frequent in the modern culture of performance measurement, risk assessment, individual blame and insistence on uniformity – all presented as objective and value-free – is the temptation to subordinate the question 'Is it right?' or 'Has it been thought through?' to questions like 'Will it work?' or 'How will it look?'

The changes described in the first part of this chapter, and which academics would describe as examples of 'late modernism', can place an increasing strain on the professional and sometimes the individual conscience of public servants, and perhaps especially those who work in criminal justice. Stress is an increasing cause of personal unhappiness and operational inefficiency. There is more pressure to do what is expected than to do what is right, less support from colleagues when a problem of conscience arises – and more temptation to give in, or look for another job, than encouragement to stand and argue the case.

A text with which to conclude is Matthew 5.14–16 (NEB):

You are light for all the world. A town that stands on a hill cannot be hidden. When a lamp is lit, it is not put under the meal-tub, but on the lamp-stand, where it gives light to everyone in the house. And you, like the lamp, must shed light among your fellows, so that, when they see the good you do, they may give praise to your Father in heaven.

References

Archbishop of Canterbury's Commission on Urban Priority Areas, *Faith in the City*. Church House Publishing, London, 1985.

Auld, Lord Justice, *Review of the Criminal Courts of England and Wales*. Stationery Office, London, 2001.

Beetham, David, *The Legitimation of Power*. Macmillan, London, 1991.

Board for Social Responsibility, *Crime, Justice and the Demands of the Gospel*. General Synod Board for Social Responsibility, London, 1991.

Bottoms, Anthony, 'Compliance and Community Penalties' in Bottoms, A., Gelsthorpe, L. and Rex, S. (eds), *Community Penalties: Change and Challenge*. Willan Publishing, Cullompton, Devon, 2001.

Burnside, Jonathan and Baker, Nicola (eds), *Relational Justice: Repairing the Breach*. Waterside Press, Winchester, 1994.

Commission on the Future of Multi-Ethnic Britain, *The Future of Multi-Ethnic Britain*. Profile Books, London, 2000.

Faulkner, David, *Crime, State and Citizen: A Field Full of Folk*. Waterside Press, Winchester, 2001.

Field-Smith, Robin, 'The Case for Police Chaplains', *Criminal Justice Management*, September 2001, pp. 34–5.

Garland, David, *The Culture of Control: Crime and Social Order in Contemporary Society*. Oxford University Press, Oxford, 2001.

Halliday, John, *Making Punishments Work*, Report of a Review of the Sentencing Framework for England and Wales. Home Office, London, 2001.

Hobbes, Thomas, *Leviathan*. 1651.

Home Office, *Policing a New Century: A Blueprint for Reform* Cm 5326. Stationery Office, London, 2001.

Hood, Roger, 'Penal Policy and Criminological Challenges in the New Millennium?', *Australian and New Zealand Journal of Criminology*, Vol. 34 No. 1, 2001, pp. 1–16.

Macpherson, Sir William, *The Stephen Lawrence Inquiry*, Cm 5262. Stationery Office, London, 1999.

Nellis, Michael, 'The New Probation Training in England and Wales: Realising the Potential', *Social Work Education*, Vol. 20 No. 4, 2001, pp. 415–32.

Newell, Tim, *Forgiving Justice: A Quaker Vision for Criminal Justice*. Quaker Home Service, London, 2000.

Neyroud, Peter and Beckley, Alan, *Policing, Ethics and Human Rights*. Willan Publishing, Cullompton, Devon, 2001.

Sparks, Richard, Bottoms, Anthony and Hay, Will, *Prisons and the Problem of Order*. Clarendon Press, Oxford, 1996.

Speller, Adrian, *Breaking Out: A Christian Critique of Criminal Justice*. Hodder and Stoughton, London, 1986.

Wright, Martin, *Restoring Respect for Justice*. Waterside Press, Winchester, 1999.

2 | The Political Debate

Juliet Lyon

Introduction

Politicians do not send offenders to prison, but they do have an important role – to influence opinion and to educate the public about crime and justice. In just over ten years, their preoccupation with so-called 'toughness' on crime has helped to create a harsher social and political climate in which the prison population in England and Wales has increased drastically.

Governments do not send offenders to prison, but they are responsible for sentencing policy, creating a framework and guidelines which, in a decade, have served to increase the use of custody for an ever-wider range of offences and to increase significantly the number of offences which carry a mandatory penalty.

In this chapter I will present an argument for the values and principles of humanity, justice and proportionality to be reintroduced into the political debate on criminal justice and for a halt to be called to the damaging adversarial politics to which we have been subjected. It is ironic that so many of our fellow citizens who are held in prison will have, in childhood, experienced inconsistent parenting, warring families, harsh and erratic discipline and a lack of proper care and supervision. The country does not need political leaders who replicate this harshness and inconsistency in policy-making in criminal justice. Instead, we look to them to lead a balanced, informed debate to help us rethink our approach to crime and punishment and create a safer society.

I will draw extensively on one such debate in the House of Lords initiated by Douglas Hurd in July 2001 to call attention to the state of our prisons. The damage caused by the scourge of overcrowding will be explored. A case will also be put for developing and promoting alternatives to custody and for protecting the vulnerable. The chapter will close with a call to reinforce and extend parliamentary and public scrutiny of our penal system.

Changing the nature of the debate

> We are almost unique among civilized countries in that we have a party political dog fight over the criminal justice system; it need not be like that. That arrangement does not benefit the population as a whole, let alone the prison population. (Lord Rooker, House of Lords 2001)

When political parties compete on toughness on crime the fall-out from the ensuing penal arms race is devastating. In a punitive climate, tens of thousands of people who have offended find themselves ratcheted up the sentencing scale to the end point of the criminal justice system. Many of them will leave our overcrowded, under-resourced prisons more, rather than less, likely to offend again. Overall, 58 per cent of prisoners and a depressing 76 per cent of young offenders will be reconvicted within two years of release.

As part of this destructive cycle, family ties are shattered and opportunities to find work or decent housing are reduced. In just one year, over 130,000 children will be affected by their fathers' imprisonment and more than 10,000 separated from their mothers. Harm is being done, and a legacy of social exclusion established, out of all proportion to the seriousness of much of the original offending. Recent opinion polls on reducing re-offending certainly do not indicate a public appetite for the increased use of imprisonment; in fact, rather the reverse.

Since 1991 the prison population in England and Wales has risen from 45,900 to over 70,000 in 2002. We now have the highest rate of imprisonment in Western Europe. This meteoric rise in prison numbers has more to do with political rhetoric on toughness on crime than with variations in the crime rate.

It is time for a different debate, a balanced debate, which has at its heart an interest in preventing the next victim rather than the assumed vote-winning and headline-catching qualities of 'crackdown' and temporary incapacitation. This debate must take the long view. It should be informed by evidence of effective work with offenders in the community as well as in the prison environment. It should refer to good practice in crime reduction and prevention in Western Europe and elsewhere. It should have the broadest possible remit to take into account the needs and characteristics of people who offend, together with the role statutory and voluntary organizations can play in providing services, supervision and support.

Public debate of this kind should involve politicians but steer clear of party politics. It must involve people who know about life in prisons: prisoners, ex-prisoners, their families and friends, prison staff and managers, voluntary and penal affairs groups and allied agencies. Sentencers have an important contribution to make. Faith groups, too often quiet on penal matters, must be there in good voice. The guiding principle should be one of inclusion. This accords with Tim Newell's view that 'the fact that we resort to prison too quickly is a reflection not of crime rates but of our inability to tolerate and embrace the "other" in our society, those who are different and difficult and require too much effort on our part to include them in our social intercourse' (Newell 2000).

The time is right to move from short-term initiatives to sustained policy-making. Interestingly, it was Tony Blair, now Prime Minister, in his role as Shadow Home Secretary in 1993 when he delivered the Perrie Lecture, who said:

> What we require is not a series of policy initiatives that are a reflex response to particular events occurring in our society, but a thought-out policy, a strategy if you like, that deals with all the various aspects of the problems that we face and doesn't attempt to isolate the Prison Service from the rest of the criminal justice system. (Blair 1993)

In places where tough rhetoric has taken root as policy it must be grubbed up. We need to heed the warning that 'The superficial attraction to the general public of proclaimed toughness is self-evident. It is infectious and quickly spreads across the political spectrum. However, it can serve as a rhetorical smokescreen, presaging the introduction of questionable policies which then come to be regarded as politically irreversible' (Windlesham 1996). Instead, a new framework should be developed which links family and social policy with criminal justice, cuts right across government departments, education, health, housing, employment, as well as the Home Office and leads to a coherent response to crime.

The cornerstones for reform of the criminal justice system are in place with Lord Justice Auld's review of the criminal courts, John Halliday's review of the sentencing framework and the Social Exclusion Unit's extensive work on preventing re-offending by ex-offenders, and a useful review of resettlement produced jointly by the Chief Inspectors of Prisons and Probation.

Importantly, adversarial lines on criminal justice policy are not deeply drawn between the main political parties. There appear to be broad areas of agreement on early intervention and support for parents, crime reduction, improvements in public services, better mental health and drug treatment, a reduction in the use of short prison sentences in favour of community programmes, and improved opportunities for intensive work with violent and persistent offenders in prison.

Unusually, perhaps uniquely, the Home Secretary, the Lord Chief Justice and the Director General of the Prison Service are shoulder to shoulder on the need to reduce prisoner numbers to an unavoidable minimum. It is a paradoxical time for prison reform. The government is committed to public service reform, together with a radical overhaul of the criminal justice system. But a tidal wave of prison numbers, a few high-profile criminal cases and a vengeful popular press or a poor showing in the spending review could yet sweep away its resolve, and with it, the future prospects of some of our most isolated citizens and damaged young people.

The state of Her Majesty's Prisons

On 11 July 2001, Lord Hurd of Westwell rose in the House of Lords to call attention to the state of our prisons. In his opening speech he said:

> We do no service to a victim by making a hash of the treatment of the offender. On the contrary, a prison which is overcrowded – as happens; a prison whose governor changes every year – as

happens; a prison run according to the culture of an outdated trade union – as happens; a prison where locking up seems to be the be all and end all of life – as happens; such a prison serves as a reservoir for future crime. In such a prison, new offences and new victims are being prepared day by day. For those reasons it is important we should have this debate. (House of Lords 2001)

This substantive debate shows how cross-party political debate can shed light on the dark, closed world of prisons. It was the last to which Bob Hardy contributed as Bishop of Prisons. Characteristically he chose to focus on the needs of the most vulnerable: the mentally ill and children and young people in prison.

One after another their Lordships rose like a cloud of witnesses to call attention to the state of our prisons, to pay tribute to the beleaguered Prison Service struggling to contain the worst overcrowding crisis on record (and now, sadly, very much worse still) and to offer wise counsel on the need for humanity and justice in policy-making to a new Home Secretary setting out to reform the criminal justice system. In so doing they drew not only on aggregated centuries of parliamentary work and political debate but also on their knowledge of what happens in prisons and their involvement with men, women and children held in these institutions and the staff charged with their care. In this way they were able to reflect on the enduring impact of imprisonment on people and their families and to present an overwhelming case for reserving prison only for those whose offending is so serious and so persistent, and who present such a grave risk to the public, that there can be no alternative to custody. Without exception, they exposed the practice of imprisoning more and more people as a matter for national shame.

In just under five hours of debate, a wide range of concerns and solutions was covered. An agenda for radical reform was developed, drawing on international comparisons, and set in a historical perspective. Members of the House explored the disastrous impact of penal populism over the years.

Overall, the debate was characterized by generosity of spirit, a determination to supersede party politics and a commitment to creating a just, effective and humane penal system. There were, of course, acknowledgements of the intractable nature of the problem, of the many futile attempts to solve it and the sheer waste of time, resources and human lives in the process.

The Lords urged David Blunkett to remain true to his resolve to drive down prison numbers and to be imaginative in his efforts to produce effective alternatives to imprisonment. The Lord Bishop of Lincoln drew his own contribution to the debate to a close with these words:

> There are two kinds of vulnerability in our world: an enforced vulnerability which hurts, breaks and is at risk in the world of the prison. Alongside there is the Christian hope . . . and the freely chosen vulnerability of love. This second kind, the vulnerability of love, involves taking risks. I hope and pray that our new Home Secretary and his ministerial team will be prepared to take some risks – risks which will break new ground and give real hope to those of us who care about our prisons. (House of Lords 2001)

The scourge of overcrowding

The damage done at every level by the scourge of prison overcrowding cannot be underestimated. Prisoners are subject to poor and unacceptable conditions. They spend excessive time locked in their cells. In a few large, overcrowded prisons, remand prisoners, who unjustly experience the worst conditions of all, are locked in for up to 22 hours a day. Increasing numbers of people are currently held two to a cell designed for one. The degrading practice of slopping out, almost eradicated by the internal sanitation programme introduced following the Woolf Report, is creeping back into a few prisons as they are forced to bring back into service wings closed down for humanitarian or health and safety reasons.

Opportunities for purposeful activity are severely curtailed. Despite tremendous efforts by the Prison Service to increase levels of activity, the hours poured in have simply been mopped up by the increasing numbers. It is a startling fact that in ten years, purposeful activity has only increased by ten minutes each day for each prisoner. It has become more difficult for prisoners to complete education courses, training for work and offending behaviour programmes as they are shunted around the prison system due to the shortage of bed spaces. These transfers, usually with little or no notice, make it very difficult for people to maintain contact with family and friends. Currently more than 11,000 people are held over 100 miles from home. Prison visits have dropped by one third in the last few years as people are held further from home, and further from the support they need to resettle in society.

The pressure of overcrowding demoralizes prison staff and contributes to exceptionally high levels of staff sickness and difficulties in recruiting and retaining good people. Coping with the burgeoning prison population preoccupies senior managers and deflects them from their own radical programme of reform to create decent prison regimes and their plans to effect a step change in rehabilitation and resettlement.

In his lecture to the Prison Reform Trust to mark the tenth anniversary of the publication of his report into the riot at Strangeways Prison, Lord Woolf, the Lord Chief Justice, was unequivocal that the scourge of prison overcrowding had proved the most significant block to reform. He expressed grave disappointment that only limited improvements had been made, given that 'We were on our way to creating a system of which the nation did not need to be ashamed and which would have made a positive contribution in the fight against crime' (Woolf 2001). He presented a clear action plan to reduce overcrowding which included increasing sentencing options and reducing sentence lengths. It is of note that sentence lengths have increased in all courts and that in the Crown Court between 1990 and 2000 the average sentence for all indictable offences increased from 17.7 to 21 months, leading to a significant increase in prison numbers. Lord Woolf concluded by calling on the government to take action:

What would have a greater effect on overcrowding than anything I can propose would be an announcement by the Government that it fully accepts the damaging effects of prison overcrowding and that it attaches highest priority to eliminating this problem. The Government could then set out a programme for containing the number of prisoners. With the overt support of the Government what has not been achieved over 30 years could now be achieved. The money, which would be saved by a reduction in numbers once the programme started, would fund a downward spiral in prison numbers to replace the upward spiral. The public

would directly benefit from a diversion of resources into programmes to tackle offending and the closely related problems of
education deficit and the culture of drug and alcohol abuse.
(Woolf 2001)

There is a general consensus that severe overcrowding stops prison
from working in any sense. However building new prisons has not
proved a solution. In the last ten years, 26 new prisons have been
opened at a cost of £100,000 per prison place. Of these new prisons, 20
are already overcrowded. It is now clear that the government should
further develop and promote community alternatives to custody for less
serious offenders in order to alleviate prison overcrowding. A new
Prisons Act must include a new Prison Rule that no prison should be
overcrowded, with provisions for Parliament to be informed if exceptionally there is to be a material departure from that rule.

Promoting alternatives to custody

If the overall public climate is a harsh one, fuelled by Ministers'
tough sounding rhetoric, the courts will respond by imprisoning
ever more offenders. If we want a balanced sentencing and penal
policy with a sparing and appropriate use of prison and a greater
use of community supervision, Ministers must go out and sell the
case just as strongly as some of their predecessors have sold the
case for harsher punishment. (Earl of Dundee, House of Lords
2001)

David Blunkett is by no means the first, but within the decade he is the
only, Home Secretary prepared to make a public commitment to reducing prison numbers and to set up a programme of government
information to explain why. In his address to the Prison Service Conference, he made it clear that he supported the finding of the Halliday
Review that short prison sentences do little or nothing to prevent
offending in the long term. He also took the commonsense view that
community sentences, particularly those with a reparative or restorative
element, work better and do not get in the way of intensive work with
those serving long custodial sentences. He said:

So, there is a message really. It's a simple message: I want to ensure that what works is actually put into practice. And if we have a situation where larger and larger groups of people are committed to custody for less than six months and if that displaces existing longer term prisoners in jails around the country whose programmes of training, adult literacy and numeracy in preparation for release are then completely disrupted and if by musical cells, because that's what it is, we dislocate the programmes that are taking place on tackling drugs offences and drugs misuse and if we make it more difficult to manage the prisoners who are in there, then we are crazy. This is a daft way to operate. (Blunkett 2002)

Talking down prison numbers will be a much more difficult task than increasing them. Michael Howard, when Home Secretary, chose to promote the effectiveness of custodial sentences. His unequivocal statements on 'prison works' propelled numbers upwards very quickly indeed. If David Blunkett is to succeed in his strategy to make prison work for serious persistent offenders by holding them securely and by providing opportunities for them to turn their lives around, then there is considerable work to be done on developing and promoting community sentences for less serious offenders so that they inspire the confidence of sentencers and the public.

There is also an important matter of timing as well as coherent policy development. Reforms to improve police performance, and court services, if successful, will propel more offenders through the criminal justice system at a faster rate, at least until increased prospects of detection become a deterrent in themselves. At the same time, the Director General of the Prison Service is understandably keen to publicize improvements in prison regimes, including the range of accredited qualifications gained by prisoners and the positive developments in drug treatment programmes (Narey 2002). However, unless, or until, prison is established as a genuine place of last resort, there are real dangers in promoting its potential to transform or rehabilitate. Surely the pain and lasting stigma of imprisonment could only be justified if the offence warranted such a serious penalty. No one in their right mind would send someone to prison to get drug treatment or to make up for educational deficits.

In the prisons debate Lord Faulkner examined some of these complexities and pitfalls:

> One unfortunate consequence of the 'prison works' philosophy is that if rehabilitation succeeds in preventing re-offending and in reforming the characters of offenders, judges and magistrates will take the view that the more people they send to gaol, the more they will benefit from the experience. What is more, they may as well increase the length of the sentences as well, because there is no point in sending people to prison unless they stay long enough to gain some benefit. Unless something can be done to improve the offender's family and social environment outside the prison, the expectations of the 'prison works' philosophy are likely to remain unrealistic and the rates of re-offending will stay depressingly high. One will then get into a thoroughly negative debate that goes along the lines of having to keep people in prison for longer and longer because that is the only place where they will not re-offend in ways that affect the population as a whole. That is just investing in failure. (Lord Faulkner of Worcester, House of Lords 2001)

Early intervention and prevention and support for vulnerable families such as that offered by the Sure Start programme promise most in regard to reducing offending in the long term. But these strategies require a Home Secretary prepared to keep a steady nerve to enlist public confidence in work which may take a generation to prove its worth. Lord Elton spoke for many when he said:

> Neither building prisons nor adjusting custodial sentences of themselves will result in any significant reduction in the criminality or in the population of the prisons or in the cost of managing them. We have to look elsewhere. That is that it is far more sensible to get the children before they become criminals than to spend enormous resources in catching 3 per cent of those who offend and then committing a small proportion to a custodial sentence which almost guarantees that they will go back and do it again. Someone coming from elsewhere in the universe would regard that as a policy of lunacy, yet we have been pursuing it, as

though hypnotised, for generation after generation. (Lord Elton, House of Lords 2001)

Protecting the vulnerable

The fact is that our prisons are still absolutely unacceptably over-crowded and the rate of increase in the prison population remains unacceptably high. We continue to incarcerate people who represent no risk to the community, people who are mentally ill and should not be in prison at all, people whose lives and relationships are already disrupted and dysfunctional, and people whose level of education means that 70 per cent have reading ages, literacy and numeracy skills lower than those of an eight-year-old – and all at the most fantastic cost. (Baroness Linklater, House of Lords 2001)

Prisons are not neutral environments. Large, closed institutions will inevitably increase dependence and reduce personal responsibility. They will increase vulnerability and reduce resilience. Imprisonment further excludes people who are isolated already and confirms them in a criminal identity. How much better then to avoid altogether the imprisonment of particularly vulnerable groups in our society.

Each time we lock up a child we must acknowledge that we have failed in our duty of care. Currently we are in danger of creating a false divide between those we define as vulnerable children in need of care and protection and those children who offend and who, due to their behaviour, we see as threatening and dangerous – not children at all but 'bail bandits' or 'terror tots' according to recent headlines. The fact is that these children are both victims and perpetrators of crime.

Undoubtedly there are a small number of children and young people who represent a risk to the public and who are themselves so out of control as to need containing and detaining. The challenge is to respond decisively and appropriately without making these vulnerable, volatile children worse. Intensive supervision and surveillance schemes, reparation, community service, involving children in solving the problems they have helped to create, all have potential (Lyon *et al.* 2000).

It is too early for a full evaluation of the work of the Youth Justice Board, but its determination not to write off children who offend as the criminals of the future and its belief that children and adolescents can change, particularly given the right kind of support and supervision, are important guiding principles.

Bob Hardy expressed the unequivocal view that 'Children should not be held in prison. It is a damaging environment and is ineffective in terms of reducing re-offending. Secure accommodation should be the only form of custody for young people and should only be used as a last resort in order to protect the public' (Lord Bishop of Lincoln, House of Lords 2001).

Just as we must work towards ending the imprisonment of children, also to protect the vulnerable we must not accept the incarceration of the mentally ill in inappropriate prison settings. A contributor to a recent Prison Reform Trust conference on responding to the mental health needs of women in prison spoke of her experience and her dependence on prescribed medication which developed at this time. She said: 'During the two and half years of my incarceration I was to discover the depths of despair one can fall into, believing I was losing my mind, believing I was dead, believing I was buried alive, believing I would never be free. I learnt about self-harm, physically and emotionally, I learnt how to survive, yet at the same time how it feels to want to die every day. I learnt that tears can keep coming for days and days and days. Prison is not a place for the mentally ill.'

Of the 4,000 women in custody in England and Wales, 40 per cent will have received mental health treatment, one in five will have been admitted as an in-patient in a psychiatric hospital, and one third will have attempted suicide at some point in their lives.

Government figures reveal shockingly poor mental health in the prison population compared with the general population. To give one example, ten per cent of sentenced young offenders suffer from a serious psychotic illness such as schizophrenia. This is 50 times the rate of mental illness experienced by young people living at home. The Prison Service, working in partnership with the NHS, is striving to improve impoverished mental health services in prisons. But the fact remains that there is a severe shortage of secure mental health beds in the NHS, and prisons continue to hold people who are far too ill to be there.

A key factor in the upsurge in the prison population was the government decision, following political debate, to close many of the large, long-stay psychiatric hospitals and to create instead a system of care in the community. The strategy failed because adequate systems of treatment and specialist support were not put in place and vulnerable people looking forward to independence found only isolation and lack of care. Significant numbers continue to find their way into the criminal justice rather than the mental health system.

It is a tribute to the courage and faith of Paul and Audrey Edwards, whose mentally ill son Christopher was murdered in Chelmsford Prison by a mentally ill prisoner, that a decision reached in the European Court of Human Rights should lead to more humane treatment for mentally disordered offenders. In a press notice issued in March 2002, they said:

> We hope that today's ECHR decision will not only achieve some justice for ourselves and our son but will establish key principles that should effect change in the criminal justice system. Firstly, mentally disordered offenders should receive appropriate medical treatment by skilled staff in a secure surrounding, rather than be warehoused in the wholly unsuitable environment of a prison without adequate mental health care. Over half of all prisoners suffer some form of mental illness and therefore this should be a major step forward. (Board for Social Responsibility 2002)

Open to scrutiny

Paradoxically, prisons are hidden, isolated places which often find themselves in the public eye. Prison staff and managers are bombarded with advice and questions from so many interested parties: prisoners and their families; politicians; civil servants; independent monitors; inspectors; penal affairs groups; voluntary organizations; and the press. Struggling to do an exceptionally difficult job, often in a bleak environment with limited resources, it must be very hard to take this level of scrutiny. But it is essential, as the Archbishop of Canterbury stated when he delivered the Prison Reform Trust lecture:

> Prisons belong to us all and are now more open to public scrutiny and ideas and other contributions from the wider society. I hope

that the Prison Service will feel sufficient self-confidence to remain open to contact and ideas from the world outside prisons. One of the worst things that can happen to any profession is to become preoccupied with the feeling of being beleaguered, misused and misunderstood. It is an occupational hazard for Archbishops, Government Ministers, policemen, teachers, social workers and not least prison officers but it must be resisted from above. (Carey 1996)

Lord Faulkner in the prisons debate emphasized the importance of taking a proper interest in prisons. He said:

There is no substitute for exposure to and involvement in the realities of prison and its alternatives. I know how much the Prison Service welcome a proper interest in their work. The impossible scale of the task demanded of them might just begin to be properly understood if more sentencers and politicians, as well as the public, became aware of those realities. What we see on TV, read in the papers or hear as soundbites from the politicians are a distorting substitute. (Lord Faulkner, House of Lords 2001)

Creating a just, humane and effective penal system is a matter for us all. There is no doubt that the debate on crime and punishment needs to be widened. The enfranchisement of prisoners, in prospect following the Human Rights Act, would be an important step forward in this regard:

The blanket ban on prisoners voting is a relic from the nineteenth century, which is neither a deterrent nor an effective punishment. Giving prisoners the vote would encourage them to take responsibilities that come with citizenship. It would also encourage politicians to take more of an active interest in prisons, which in turn would raise the level of debate about prisons and penal policy. (Levenson 2001)

There can be no doubt that the political debate must be informed by the recognition that there is a common humanity shared by people on either side of the prison gates. Justice, not vengeance, must be at the heart of this debate, together with a belief in people's capacity to change and a preparedness to help them do so. Once prison takes its rightful place, as one of absolute last resort in a reformed criminal justice system, then, and only then, can we expect it to work.

References

Blair, T., Prison Service Perrie Lecture, 1993, in Reynolds, J. and Smartt, U. (eds), 'Prison Policy and Practice', *Prison Service Journal.* Leyhill, 1996.

Blunkett, D., Address to Prison Service Conference, 2002.

Board for Social Responsibility, *Prisons: A Study in Vulnerability,* Church House Publishing, London, 1999.

Carey, G., *Restoring Relationships: The Purpose of Prison.* Prison Reform Trust, London, 1996.

House of Lords, Debate on the State of Our Prisons. Hansard, London, 11 July 2001.

Levenson, J., *Barred from Voting.* Prison Reform Trust, London, 2001.

Lyon, J., Dennison, C. and Wilson, A., *Tell Them So They Listen: Messages from Young People in Custody,* Home Office Research Study 201. London, 2000.

Narey, M., Address to Prison Service Conference, 2002.

Newell, T., *Forgiving Justice: a Quaker Vision for Criminal Justice.* Quaker Home Service, London, 2000.

Windlesham, Lord, *Responses to Crime, Volume 3: Legislating with the Tide.* Clarendon Press, Oxford, 1996.

Woolf, Lord, *Strangeways Ten Years On.* Prison Reform Trust, London, 2001.

3 | **An Inclusive Legal System**

Helena Kennedy

LAW'S PURPOSE is to regulate social relations by creating a set of rules. But law can do more than that. It can be one of the instruments in a society which transmits values from one generation to another and can help create what Justice Felix Frankfurter, the American judge, called 'that continuity of a treasured common life'.

In all societies the impulse towards order has meant the development of legal systems, which have become more complex as our world has developed and changed. Members of an organized community need to share common goals and aspirations. Lord Devlin, our own great jurist, described this mortar as 'the invisible bonds which hold a society together', and it is these values which inform the nature of our laws. Unlike rules of ethics, rules of law have to be capable of enforcement through institutions created for that purpose: courts, tribunals, adjudication panels, police forces, bailiffs, prisons, probation services and so on. There has been continuing debate over the years about whether the law should enforce morals, and the growing consensus is that this is not the law's purpose. However, while it is not law's role to be morally coercive, a set of principles and values should underpin the law and act as a touchstone for the way in which legal systems work. The law itself should be moral.

We have come a long way from the days when the Magisterium, the Church's teaching authority, could set absolute parameters for morality, not unlike the way Sharia law still does in some nations, with clear rules and fixed responses to breaches of them. The arrival of Luther and his assertions as to the role of personal conscience changed all that for ever, reshaping moral philosophy, history and ultimately law. The struggle between subjective and objective morality is ongoing – indeed, the

English legal system often invokes the test of the reasonable man (now assiduously referred to as the reasonable person!) in an effort to conjoin the subjective test for certain behaviour with objective standards.

Judeo-Christian values are an inevitable and historic part of law in Britain, whether English or Scots law. The moral horizons of lawmakers have been embedded in that tradition. Jürgen Habermas described this in his 1992 work *Postmetaphysical Thinking: Philosophical Essays*: 'We as Europeans cannot seriously understand concepts like morality and ethical life, person and individuality, or freedom and emancipation without appropriating the substance of the Judeo-Christian understanding of history in terms of salvation.'

While most of our laws did not get there simply by virtue of being Christian, there is no doubt that Christian morality laid the foundation and flavoured the judgements in our courts. We believe in monogamy as a moral principle, and our law reflects it. The right of men to have more than one wife would be inimical now not just for religious reasons but because of women's expectations of equality. In Islamic societies the law may reflect Islamic values, but Muslims in Britain have to conform to British laws.

However, over a century ago the courts rejected the idea that 'Christianity is parcel of the laws of England' (Regina *v* Ramsey and Foot, 1883, Cox CC), conscious of the problems such an assertion would create in a society already becoming more secular. But law cannot be a value-free zone or just be pragmatic. Nor can it be based upon a notion currently very popular with the government, 'What is right is what works'. There has to be a ground soil from which the law springs; there have to be principles. Lawmaking cannot be *ad hoc*, made up on the spot to deal with contingencies as they arise, as seemed to be the case in the response to the tragic events of 11 September in the United States. The Rule of Law is one of the central building blocks of a safe and civilized world.

The question which must be posed now is: what are the values which should underpin the law in a society which is no longer homogeneous?

The law issues messages which resonate throughout society, and those messages are internalized. It tells a woman whether she really is equal to a man; it tells the black citizen whether his rights are as protected as those of his white brother; it tells the poor whether their rights of redress are just the same as those of the rich. Today more than ever it is essential that in securing confidence in the law we ensure that the principles underlying the law are ones which are shared by the majority of citizens. How do we identify shared values when our society has become so diverse, with people of so many different cultures becoming part of our social fabric?

In reality, many of the values of Christians overlap with those of non-Christians, whether they are atheists, agnostics or people of other religions. There are also profoundly valuable concepts from other traditions, which would enrich our own. Responsibility and respect for elders seems to be far more entrenched in the Muslim tradition than in ours. It is important in respecting cultural difference that we recognize, for example, that formal adoption is anathema to Islam and contrary to religious law, while fostering and caring for orphaned or abandoned children is seen as part of religious duty. However, there are also traditions and practices in immigrant communities which could never be acceptable in contemporary Britain and should always be outlawed – from forced marriages to female circumcision, from the failure to send girls to school to the incitement of *jihad* or holy war.

But what are the core principles which must be the essence of the law? How do we create a system which has the confidence and trust of the public, a system which is inclusive and which all people feel is theirs?

When people are asked in the National Census or other research how they view the legal system, they invariably say that the system is weighted in favour of the rich and privileged. They also believe that the system discriminates, particularly against black people. They believe on the one hand that innocent people are wrongly convicted, but they also believe that guilty people get away with it. There is distrust of police and lawyers alike, and the perception is that the courts are not in touch with the reality of people's lives.

This distrust of the legal system has serious consequences for society because our social well-being depends upon a social contract which has observance of the law at its heart. Citizens agree to take their grievances through the courts rather than secure redress or compensation in less satisfactory ways. They agree to take their wrongs to the police rather than exact punishment directly. Once people decide that the legal system is way too costly, unjust or prejudiced there is serious erosion of one of the central pillars of our democracy.

The problem is that not everyone will be happy with the legal system all of the time. The law is always about competing interests. Those who lose their actions for damages and end up with a costs bill are never happy. Those who commit crimes frequently are disgruntled about the consequent punishment. Victims almost invariably feel that the system leaves them on the sidelines and often believe the sentence passed on an offender is insufficient. In the divorce courts, women still perceive the scales as falling down more favourably on the financial front for their former husbands, but men feel women get an unfair advantage on the custody of children. In the legal system people win and others lose, which means that total contentment is illusory. In criminal law, there is a constant tension between the needs of those who suffer crime and those who are accused of it, and it is within that tension that justice is defined.

What is clear, however, is that there has to be a regular fine-tuning of the law to a changing world, and a willingness to shed preconceptions. The law can never be out of step with public opinion or it will be held in contempt, but neither can it respond to every editorial in the tabloid newspapers or it could become manipulated by our worst impulses. This two-step which the law has to conduct, of leading public opinion yet also reflecting it, is a difficult manoeuvre, but what does not work is for the system to dismiss public concerns out of hand.

Law reform is never easy, but it should always be conducted against a backdrop of principle, with a clear sense of those things which are not negotiable, the principles which are inviolable. On a recent visit to the United States people were aghast when I explained that, in Britain, judges could now invite a jury to draw an adverse inference from the accused refusing to answer questions or not testifying. For Americans, the right to silence is one of those inviolable principles. 'Taking the Fifth', or relying on the Fifth Amendment of the Constitution, is the citizen's protective cloak against potential state abuse.

The principles

For me, the basic principles which should underlie the legal system are equality before the law, fairness, and respect for human dignity. It is difficult to see how a society could remain open and democratic while consciously disavowing any obligation to act nondiscriminately, fairly and in ways which respect the essential humanity of an individual. Yet our system still fails those tests in certain respects.

Law in England by its very nature evolves, and it is seen as one of its great strengths that it develops by accretion rather than being locked into a written constitution or legal code. There are three strands in our law's creation. Law is made by judges in the courts, so that a body of case-law develops upon which they draw for guidance as they deliberate – this is at the heart of the Common Law system. There is also law created by statute in Parliament after amendments, debate and voting. The other contribution to lawmaking is the academic work of respected legal commentators in our universities whose work is cited in legal argument in the courts. The nature of law's creation meant that until very recently the law was being made by white men and from a white male perspective. There was no conscious conspiracy of men in long wigs, but women and ethnic minorities were not represented in the ranks of judges who were making law, nor were they present in Parliament in significant numbers nor in the high echelons of academe. For example, it was only in 1991 that the Law Lords rejected the long held legal premise that however a husband acted sexually with his wife, it was legally not to be accounted as rape. It had been based upon outmoded notions of wifely subservience, and the court decided, not before time, that the law had to move on. Their decision was undoubtedly affected by the widespread discontent from the Women's Institute through to the Union of Catholic Mothers that domestic violence was a serious issue not being addressed by the courts.

From the early 1970s onwards the women's movement had turned its spotlight on the legal system and its failure to secure justice for women in many areas, from employment and family matters through to their experience as victims in the courts, especially in rape trials and cases involving domestic abuse. As a result of women's critique of the system, much change has taken place. However, in rape cases the conviction rate remains the lowest in all areas of crime. Only one in 13 cases results in a conviction. Domestic violence still remains one of the most prevalent violent offences.

The legal profession itself has undertaken reform and is seeking to eliminate discrimination against women, but the numbers of women on the Bench, particularly in the higher courts, is still abysmally low. The recent appointments to the position of Queen's Counsel included 101 men and only 12 women. Since it is from the pool of silks that High Court judges will be drawn, it will be many a long year before women are there in significant numbers.

The issue of race also remains highly contentious in legal circles, with many lawyers, judges and magistrates unwilling to accept that the colour of a person's skin in any way affects their judgements. This is true even if it is suggested that their approach may be unconscious or indirect. Many see racial disadvantage as rooted in society, requiring a political resolution outside the province of the court. They describe their function in a mechanistic way, involving the application of the law as an impartial set of rules to be applied without fear or favour regardless of gender, colour or creed.

Yet something does go wrong. Although black people constitute just six per cent of the population they make up disproportionate percentages of the prison population, at times as high as 28 per cent. Since social deprivation is linked to criminal behaviour it is not surprising that black people should end up in prison in higher numbers. However, persuasive research shows that this alone cannot account for the discrepancy. There are, of course, those who choose to interpret the figures as proof of black criminality; such crude views defy contradiction or rational debate. What seems to happen is that all along the criminal justice journey, black people are likely to encounter discrimination – from wrongful arrests to over-charging, readier refusals of bail, or higher sentences.

The Stephen Lawrence case alerted everyone to the issues of institutional racism, and no institution can count itself exempt. Every part of the legal system should be reviewing its practices and its failures to be inclusive. The police have set targets for the recruitment of black trainees but in the legal profession there is no shortage of able young graduates from the ethnic minorities entering the law. However, the numbers of black senior practitioners and judges can be counted on the fingers of one hand, perhaps now two. Historic disadvantage experienced by minorities makes the pool of older black lawyers small, but wonderful people are coming through quickly and the case for a bit of fast-tracking in judicial appointments is unarguable in my view.

Victims

The position of victims within our system is still parlous. Although in recent years agencies of victim support have come into being and attempts are being made to ameliorate the experience of witnesses in court, there is still insufficient sensitivity to the needs of victims within the system. When I first started in practice, prosecuting counsel was not even allowed to pass the time of day with a Crown witness in case it was suggested that he or she was coaching the witness or behaving in a way inconsistent with the role of independent prosecutor. Now that has all changed, and at least a terrified rape victim is introduced to the person 'on her side'. There is now talk of introducing specialist counsel to deal with sexual offences, and I have long held the view that not only should specialist teams undertake rape prosecutions as in other jurisdictions, but there should also be similar specialist teams for cases involving offences against children. In every serious offence a family liaison officer is appointed at the earliest stage to keep people informed at every stage of the investigation and proceedings. There are many more ways in which the needs of victims can be addressed, and the 'restorative justice system', which emanates from New Zealand and is currently being piloted in certain youth offending areas here in Britain, provides many possible ways in which a victim could feel more engaged with the process.

However, although I have been a champion of victims' rights in the courts for many years and feel that we must constantly seek ways to ensure that those who have had traumatic experiences of crime are given every consideration possible, it is important that we do not allow the victim to be used as a Trojan horse to remove defendants' rights. Justice for victims cannot be bought at the expense of justice for defendants. What victims deserve is justice, which means the right person convicted on proper evidence and duly punished. Wrongful convictions do no service to victims.

In recent years, despite a whole series of publicly recognized miscarriages of justice, we have seen a sustained attack by governments upon the rights of the accused, assuming this will play well with the public. The call is for a levelling of the playing field between those accused of crime and those who have been the victims of crime. What is forgotten is that, in the social contract which underpins the criminal law, the victim hands over his or her grievance to the state. Then the state, with all its might and power, brings its full authority and all its resources to bear on the individual in a prosecution. It is for this reason that protections exist for those accused of crime. There is no equality of arms between the power of the state and the accused in the dock. There is no level playing field because the state has so much on its side. The protections which exist do so because of the well-recognized disadvantage that every accused person labours under – they stand accused. Their liberty is in jeopardy. Their reputation and chances in life thereafter will be profoundly affected if found guilty.

In the recent attempts by government to reduce the right to jury trial there were three reasons given for the reform. First, guilty people play the system and choose jury trial to waste time. The problem here is how you decide in advance of trial who the guilty people are. Second, it would save money, a rationale which would justify dispensing with trial altogether; and the third was that it would speed up the legal processes and this was in the interest of victims. Again we were seeing the hijacking of victims to spin the unacceptable into something to be relished. In fact, the government wanted jury trial to remain for the respectable person who fell foul of the law but thought it should be restricted for old lags. The principle of equality before the law was being flouted in the plans. And what the government had not realized was that the right to jury trial struck an atavistic cord with the public. This was an assault upon something cultural and, of course, law is cultural. It has its roots in who we are and in the 'treasured common life' which defines us. The House of Lords defeated the proposal twice.

Now there is talk of abandoning the double jeopardy rule so that the accused can be re-tried if acquitted and also the suggestion that juries should be told of any previous convictions the accused might have. At first sight it seems quite reasonable to non-lawyers that if a person can appeal against conviction, the Crown should be able to appeal against acquittal, especially if new evidence comes to light. The suggestion is that only a set of senior judges would decide if there should be a re-trial after acquittal and only then if the new evidence was of an extraordinary nature. The problem is that such cases would inevitably be highly publicized and notorious: victims would campaign for re-trials; tabloid newspapers would come out in support. Where would you find a jury unaffected by the fact that a set of senior judges thought that the new evidence was so compelling they would overturn a previous acquittal? The principle of fairness is immediately breached.

Yet it goes back to the reasons for providing protections – the state is not always benign. We are fortunate to live in times when we can feel sanguine, as though we really do believe that we have reached the end of history. It may be hard to imagine a fascist state or a state capable of tyranny. What we are sold is the idea that the modern state, now washed clean of ideological conflict, is even-handed, an arbiter between citizens, incapable in its managerial manifestations of any serious abuses of citizens' rights. We are told that there are procedures, appeal processes and opportunities to sue in abundance if things go wrong.

The drivers of the modern state are cost effectiveness and 'pragmatism' – and, of course, the Human Rights Act is evoked as the new mopper-up of the occasional failure or abuse of power by a state functionary. Civil liberties in this brave new world are outmoded and an encumbrance if you want to reform the legal system, save money, speed up the timetable or get more convictions. But to really understand civil liberties we have to understand the nature of power. Although the modern state may present itself differently in some respects, its essential elements remain the same. It is in the very nature of power that it has a huge capacity for corrupting. Those who acquire power find it addictive and seek even unconsciously to extend it. The state's powers, therefore, have to be held in check in the interests of the citizen. Carefully calibrated checks and balances are created down the centuries – and for good reason. Tyranny does not just come in a uniform; it also comes in an open-neck shirt and an Armani suit.

The removal of civil liberties by governments is not new. The public is always sold them on the basis that they are designed to convict the guilty, and decent citizens have nothing to fear. The rhetoric of all governments who reduce civil liberties is that they are doing so for good reason in the interests of the people and to counter disruptive elements in society. The current rhetoric, as I have explained, is that change is necessary in the interests of victims.

Civil liberties are often characterized as the preoccupation of Hampstead liberals, but all of us are ultimately affected when there are erosions. Being on the side of liberty does not mean being on the side of those who commit crime. Civil liberties are part of the glue in our society. Interfering with it exacts a serious price in the form of alienation and loss of trust.

Civil justice

Social inclusion in the legal system has to mean equal access to justice. For the most part, those accused of crime are well served in Britain, with legal aid available for anyone accused of offences other than the most trivial. A contribution is made according to means.

Since 1949, legal aid has also been paid for legal representation for litigants in civil actions with a good case who satisfied a means test. Originally covering about 70 per cent of the population, successive governments increased the stringency of the means test to reduce coverage only to people on welfare benefits and very low incomes. This was largely because litigation was becoming not only more expensive but more prevalent. As society has become better informed and educated and as people have become more conscious of their rights they have turned to the law more readily for remedies. Divorce has also increased considerably. In addition, we have become a much more consumerist society and a compensation culture has developed when services or commodities do not fulfil our higher expectations. However, the Access to Justice Act 1999 has now abolished legal aid for personal injury claims altogether and for the first time introduced a cash limited fund. This means that legal aid is no longer a right: claims will be accepted only if there are sufficient funds available and the case has sufficient priority over other cases. Litigants may find their applications rejected in the future because they have applied at the wrong time of the year or in the wrong area or fallen foul of priorities set by the area or the fund.

Other sources of funding have developed alongside the legal aid scheme. A major benefit offered by trade unions to its members has been to pay for legal representation, mainly for personal injury claims. Similarly, legal expenses insurance policies have been developed, often as an optional extra to household contents policy. Such schemes are poorly established, cover a narrow range of claims and, even where cover applies, usually have a fixed level of cover (around £50,000). The concern by many is that the new arrangements are now very complex and a deterrent to a poor person who should be able to take a case through the courts.

The most recent development in the funding of civil cases is conditional fees. The general position under English law has always been that lawyers may not be paid on the basis of agreements where lawyers were paid nothing if the case was lost, but received a higher 'success fee' if the claim succeeded. This prohibition remains for contingency fees (where the lawyer, US style, fixes their success fee as a proportion of the claimant's damages). However, through a statutory quirk, lawyers have always been permitted to offer contingency fee deals to clients with claims before the Employment Tribunal.

In contrast, conditional fee agreements (CFAs), where the lawyer fixes their fee by reference to amount of work done plus an uplift calculated as a percentage of their normal fee (rather than by reference to damages), have been lawful since implementation of the Courts and Legal Services Act 1990. Initially CFAs were limited to personal injury, insolvency, and European Court claims, but they have now been extended to include all civil (non-family) claims.

Because of the costs rules, where the loser normally pays the other side's costs, claimants almost always need insurance before they can pursue a case under CFAs. Affordable policies are normally available for cases with high prospects of success; but in cases where prospects of success are more uncertain, or are expensive to investigate, insurance is either not available or very expensive. Try getting insurance if you are a young black man who has in the past had some scrapes with the law.

The recent extension of CFAs, and provisions enabling successful claimants to recover insurance premiums and success fees from their opponents, have been designed to compensate for some of the decline in legal aid. Nevertheless there are serious 'funding gaps' where cases are unlikely to be funded by CFAs or the legal aid scheme. Personal injury cases with reasonable, though not 'very high' prospects of success will fall outside of the scheme and will not be backed by an insurer. These are also generally excluded from the Community Legal Service (CLS) fund which supports local advice and law centres. Other cases may fall foul of the Legal Service Commission's strict cost benefit or public interest tests but nevertheless raise substantial issues for the litigants involved, especially if the CLS funds are under pressure. There are two situations in particular which merit closer scrutiny. The first of these is the funding of group actions for damages claims. The second is dealing with public interest cases brought *pro bono* (especially on behalf of voluntary organizations).

Legal aid costs were spiralling out of control and ways had to be found to rein in the expense. However, these changes to the funding of the legal system raise serious issues about equality and access to the law. It is still early days, but there should be close monitoring of new arrangements to see who gains and who loses.

The profession

An inclusive legal system has to be served by an inclusive legal profession. In the 1970s and 1980s there was an exciting burgeoning of opportunities for young people from non-privileged backgrounds to enter the law, and I consider myself one of the lucky ones. However, the removal of grants in higher education and the introductions of fees and a loan system is proving a serious disincentive to the children of less well-to-do families. The long haul of study for legal practice, usually five to six years for those who have no possibility of family support, is driving out many potential candidates from poorer homes. The professions are themselves trying to make scholarships and financed traineeships available, but the cloud of debt frightens off many of those who are already tentative about entering a world so full of uncertainties.

Juries

It is impossible to speak about an inclusive legal system without giving proper recognition to the role of juries in securing that inclusiveness. Increasingly there is talk about the ways in which people are withdrawing from civic engagement. Fewer people vote, participate in local politics or even stand for Parliament. There is fear expressed that social capital, which is so important to the well-being of society and which comes from social engagement, is being eroded. People no longer take part in community activities. All the talk is of rights, goes the complaint, with little emphasis on duties.

Yet here we have direct involvement of members of the public in the administration of justice. The jury tradition is not just about the right of citizens to elect trial but also about the juror's duty of citizenship. It gives people an important role as stakeholders in the criminal justice system. Seeing the courts in action and participating in that process maintains public trust and confidence in the law. Perhaps we should be taking steps to strengthen the system, with fewer opportunities to avoid service and even wider participation than at present.

For the last few years I have had the privilege of chairing one of Britain's great institutions, the British Council. The Council's work is largely invisible to British eyes because it is undertaken overseas, building long-term relationships in the national interest, promoting the whole of devolved Britain through our culture – including the arts, science, education and the law. Building bridges between people of different cultures is the Council's recognized skill and has made it the most effective cultural agency in the world.

As the Cold War ended and globalization gained momentum, the emerging democracies sought to create legal systems which respected the rule of law and which inspired confidence in potential economic partners. There was little likelihood of foreign companies entering deals if there were no remedies for non-compliance. Because of the trust created through our work in education, English-language teaching and the arts, many countries turned to Britain and the Council when embracing legal reform. As a result we have been engaged in many programmes of institutional reform in China, Russia and many other parts of the former Soviet Union as well as Africa. Although our work often begins with the introduction of commercial law and intellectual property law, it frequently moves on to human rights and compliance with international norms and conventions.

It always makes me feel proud when I see the esteem in which the British legal systems and legal professionals are held and I am saddened when I watch us being cavalier with that tradition, unpicking it at the seams. This is not an argument for avoiding reform. We must always be prepared and willing to renovate the system and embrace new challenges, but we should also be clear about the central core, the essence of the system that makes it work. For a long time people have felt that the law belonged to men in wigs or people with power. It is time we made people feel that the law is theirs and that justice is indeed possible.

4 | Punishment and Justice

Christopher Jones

W HY SHOULD CHURCHES – that is, their members, leaders and theologians – be concerned with the future of criminal justice? There is a long-standing 'philanthropic' commitment of Christian people to the welfare of those in prison, which is often justified on the basis of Jesus's words in Matthew 25.36, 43: 'I was in prison and you visited me [or visited me *not*].' Since the late eighteenth century, as traced in William Noblett's chapter in this book, official expression of Christian influence in prisons has been provided by the activity of chaplains; and in the late nineteenth century, Christian involvement in the after-care of prisoners led to the incorporation of what has become the Probation Service into the criminal justice system. Such involvement can be, and in conservative theological traditions often is, understood primarily as ministry to individuals, and the institutional environment of such work may place constraints upon critical engagement with the policies to which individuals are subjected. Nevertheless, the role of prison chaplains, of various Christian denominations and now of different faiths, indicates a broader responsibility to reflect critically upon the nature and effects of the structures within which they operate. Beyond the prison walls and the boundaries of the criminal justice professions, the leaders of churches have been increasingly moved to comment upon the implications for society of the way in which crime and its perpetrators are dealt with. As a result of their historic presence within a system to which general access is restricted, churches are well placed to do this, and the existence of a Bishop to Prisons belonging to the established Church is one of the public symbols of this involvement.

The other major factor which justifies this concern is the content and orientation of the Christian message itself, which not only motivates work with individuals but provokes fundamental exploration of issues of principle and practice raised by the functioning – and mal-functioning – of a criminal justice system. For a very long time the dominant media in our society have defined response to crime in terms of punishment, and punishment in terms of imprisonment, with the result that the circle of argument narrows into a short-sighted discussion of means and far too much is taken for granted about ends. The 'justification of punishment' is a hoary old chestnut which takes the existing penal system as given and rehearses some rather tired controversies between theories of retribution, deterrence and rehabilitation.[1] Practitioners in the field are well aware that this classical paradigm no longer carries conviction either pragmatically in describing how the criminal justice process works or normatively in prescribing how it ought to work. Yet the search for a better way is elusive, and one of the major obstacles to adequate exploration is the widespread identification of justice with retribution, with offenders getting their 'just deserts' and 'paying' for their crimes. In this chapter I argue that penal policy requires the re-examination of assumptions about justice, and in particular that Christians must proceed in the light of 'what the Gospel understands by justice'.[2]

But why should there be a gulf between Christian and popular assumptions about justice, given the huge influence of Christian theology on the criminal justice systems of the nation-states which succeeded mediaeval Christendom? The answer can only be that Christian theology has at certain points lost its way in applying 'what the Gospel understands by justice' to the ordering of society. To begin to understand this regression, we need to grasp the salient features of 'justice' and 'righteousness' as envisaged in the Old and New Testaments, and the contrast between the respective concepts of justice operative in the Bible and in moral and political philosophy.

In the ancient world as in the modern, 'justice' was a many-sided and complex ideal. At the heart of it was the principle of giving people their due, but this could be understood in a variety of ways. At its simplest, it described the just person, marked by moral integrity and a sense of fairness, and by analogy it characterized institutions and communities which rightly ordered the complex web of human claims and obligations. One might call this an 'embodied' sense of justice, concretely manifesting just actions. In the *Republic*, Plato presents justice as the harmonious functioning of the diverse parts of a whole, whether this be the individual soul with its constituent elements, or the political community with its distinct classes (the links here with the political metaphor of the 'body', and with St Paul's vision of 'the body of Christ', are obvious).

On the other hand, philosophers also sought more abstract definitions of justice, trying to define the essential content of just actions and just institutions. Here the two most popular concepts, expounded influentially by Aristotle and each founded on the axiom of just deserts, were *distributive* justice, which requires that people be treated equally except insofar as their situation gives rise to unequal deserts, and *retributive* or *corrective* justice, which requires that wrongdoers be visited with a penalty appropriate and proportionate to their wrongdoing. These concepts are obviously central to any notion of social justice, but their very abstractness draws attention to the need for contextualization and interpretation: as one might say, justice requires the exercise of judgement, and cannot simply be deduced from highly generalized principles. This draws attention to the nature of justice as an active process, *doing* justice, which is very much at the heart of biblical thinking on the subject.

The word 'justice' is derived from *iustitia,* a Latin translation of terms which are prominent in the Hebrew Bible and in the New Testament, where they were translated into Greek. This results in a somewhat complex semantic structure centred on the concept of 'right', as a result of which English usage hovers between the words 'justice' and 'righteousness' without quite grasping the unity of the two and their grounding in judicial processes. The further consequence of this unclarity is that the link is easily lost between 'justice' and 'justification',[3] a key term in the thought of St Paul, and also used crucially in Jesus's parable of the Pharisee and the tax collector (Luke 18.9–14 – see especially verse 14). The attempt to 'set out what the Gospel understands by justice' depends upon re-establishing and exploring these connections.

If we have to formulate some generalizations about justice in the Old Testament, they might run along these lines. Justice, or righteousness, is not so much conformity to an abstract standard as the behaviour appropriate to God and human beings in their covenant relationship. It includes both fairness and the execution of judgement upon wrongdoing, but it goes beyond them. Righteousness and justice have their source in God and are expressed in his actions towards his people, in salvation and judgement. There is a moral basis to justice in that God vindicates the righteous and puts to shame evildoers; in that sense salvation and judgement may be two sides of the same coin. There is also the sense that God's justice is corrective, not merely in condemning and punishing wrongdoing, but in rescuing and rewarding those who do right, and even in showing mercy to those who do not deserve it. God's righteousness is entwined with faithfulness and steadfast love, qualities which do not simply treat others according to desert but look beyond failure and betrayal to forgiveness and restoration. God is not bound or limited by the flawed response of his human creatures. In that sense divine justice is creative and not merely reactive, capable of bringing about new possibilities rather than merely confirming the truth of the past.

The other pole of Old Testament thinking is that human beings may participate in God's righteousness to the extent that they act justly and in accordance with God's character. The Davidic king is the classic example of this as the guardian of the divine ordering of society and the faithful application of the law. Psalm 72 portrays his calling as the defender of the poor, the needy and the oppressed against the injustice and violence of their enemies. Individuals and nations can also share in the divine righteousness as their relationships and actions are shaped increasingly by the all-encompassing peace and just dealing of God's rule. So righteousness and justice become both critical and aspirational norms for societies, as prevailing social practice is confronted with the character of God's action in putting right wrongs and making good what has been damaged by evil – broadly, what Christian theology has come to describe as 'redemption', and modern policy-making has discovered at the level of human relationships as 'restorative justice'.

The New Testament writings bear witness to an expansion and reorientation of this experience of the redemptive or restorative aspect of divine justice. Any tendency in the old covenant to see reward and punishment as strictly symmetrical outcomes of a divine process of treating people according to their deserts is swept aside by the priority of grace in the ministry of Jesus Christ and the life of the early Church. Here the language of 'justification' is of considerable importance, because it expresses in a new context and with new intensity the relational event of

God accepting the undeserving with 'indiscriminate welcome' and transforming hospitality. Yet the means of setting right what has gone wrong is finally an act of costly self-giving which refuses to join the cycle of violence and retaliation and absorbs evil rather than returning it. And the consequence of that act of self-giving by God in Jesus is the formation of a community defined by the reality of justification and the pattern of non-retaliation – a community where the fruits of righteousness can grow, where justice is embodied in action and relationships.

Martin Luther is famous for his discovery of the Pauline teaching on justification by faith alone, and he expresses precisely the distinction made above between justice as treatment strictly according to desert, and justice as a creative setting right and renewal of relationships. In recounting his struggle to interpret the phrase 'the righteousness of God' in the Epistle to the Romans, he later wrote:

> I hated this word 'righteousness of God', which by the customary use of all the doctors I had been taught to understand philosophically as what they call the formal or *active* righteousness whereby God is just and punishes unjust sinners . . . I began to understand that . . . what Paul means is this: the righteousness of God, revealed in the Gospel, is *passive*, that is, in other words that by which the merciful God justifies us through faith.[4]

Yet Luther restricted the operative sphere of justification and passive righteousness very deliberately to the consciousness of the individual Christian and the fellowship of the Church. The redemptive justice of a merciful God was acknowledged to govern the life of faith but not the life of society. A strict distinction was maintained between God's rule over believers by means of the Gospel and his rule over the unredeemed world through the Law, administered by temporal rulers by means of coercion and punishment. In the contemporary context of social and political instability, occasioned (ironically) partly by his own reforming activities, Luther stressed the necessity of legal and penal control as a bulwark against anarchy and a restraint upon evil, to the point of commending ruthlessness in the enforcement of the law against political rebels. Whereas from earliest times Christians had pressed the claims of mercy and clemency upon secular rulers, and treated punishment as a tragic necessity, Luther's dualism had the long-term effect of insulating criminal justice from theological and moral criticism, and reinforcing the tendency to equate justice and punitive action. His complementary teaching, that Christians should embrace their social obligations and responsibilities with their outlook and motivation transformed by the knowledge of Jesus Christ, was all too easily laid aside.

An equally important influence upon the thinking of the magisterial Reformers, especially Calvin, was the analogy between the sovereign ruler and God as the source of law and executor of judgement, in which theology both reflected and reinforced political authority. Their gratitude for the mercy of God in his atoning action in Christ was framed by a strong sense of divine majesty affronted by sin and requiring satisfaction through punishment. Calvin declared as an axiom, 'God's wrath and curse always lie upon sinners until they are absolved of guilt. Since he is a righteous Judge, he does not allow his law to be broken without punishment, but is equipped to avenge it'.[5] Although Calvin was at pains to emphasize that God's love precedes and grounds his gracious acceptance of sinners, he advanced what might be called a 'pedagogy of fear':

> since our hearts cannot, in God's mercy, either seize upon life ardently enough or accept it with the gratefulness we owe, unless our minds are first struck and overwhelmed by fear of God's wrath and by dread of eternal death, we are taught by Scripture to perceive that apart from Christ, God is, so to speak, hostile to us, and his hand is armed for our destruction.[6]

This austere and guilt-shadowed concept of God clearly shares something of the intimidating character of the rulers of the time, and helps account for the dissonance in mainline Protestantism between merciful and punitive portrayals of God. When linked to the threat of eternal punishment, it produced the extraordinary combination (to which Tim Gorringe has drawn attention in the career of the Wesleys[7]) of evangelical fervour and moral insensitivity: of rejoicing in the conversion of penitent sinners on the threshold of the gallows while remaining complacent towards to the cruelties and injustices of capital punishment as then practised. As Richard Snyder has recently argued, the 'individualization of redemptive grace' denies human solidarity in both sin and redemption, and encourages the refusal of collective responsibility for the operation of the penal system.[8] There can be no separation between divine mercy and divine judgement; nor should criminal justice be isolated from 'what the Gospel understands by justice'. If God characteristically exercises mercy and wills redemption for sinners, Christians must seek to work out the implications of the divine purpose in the way in which society deals with offences and offenders.

The punitive beliefs of the magisterial Reformers reflected, in part, their positive attitude to the 'godly princes' who promoted and defended their religious reforms. Among those who experienced the governing authorities and their laws as oppressive and hostile, a different set of theological priorities took shape. Luther's dualism of Law and Gospel, retributive justice and merciful justification, was counterbalanced in the 'Radical Reformation' by the attempt to assimilate all social interaction to the tenets of the Gospel. The Mennonite and, later, the Quaker traditions in particular upheld an ethic of non-violence and rejected all forms of coercion, including judicial punishment. This approach is continued today by an influential school of biblical interpretation, pioneered by Howard Zehr in his book *Changing Lenses*[9] and now reinforced by the impressive work of Christopher Marshall on the New Testament, *Beyond Retribution* (2001).[10] According to this school, divine justice must be understood as restorative rather than punitive, and therefore human systems of justice should switch from viewing their task through what Zehr calls a 'retributive lens' to using a 'restorative lens', moving from blame-fixing to problem-solving; from a focus on the past to a focus on the future; from responding to harm by imposing a balancing harm to a response of making right.

This approach is partly a critique of retribution as the principal objective in dealing with offenders, and partly a critique of 'state justice' as it has evolved in modern societies – though it diagnoses a close connection between the two, as is shown by Zehr's appeal to 'community justice' as an alternative paradigm. Crime is viewed through the retributive lens as a violation of the State and its laws, and therefore as something of an abstraction, whereas it is viewed through the restorative lens as a violation of people and relationships. Advocates of restorative justice rightly point out that the biblical grounding of justice in the divine covenant keeps relational considerations central, and transcends the division between criminal and civil law which characterizes developed legal systems. Thus the restorative lens not only keeps in view the victims of crime – which is widely agreed to be a major weakness of existing systems of criminal justice – but seeks to do justice by 'making right' through restitution or reparation and not merely by punishing. Against the tendency of the retributive model to make the state the sole agent in administering justice, with both offenders and victims in a passive role, the restorative approach seeks to give both offenders and victims a measure of responsibility for seeking a positive resolution.[11]

Restorative justice has in recent years proved powerful both in reframing principles and reforming practice. It has offered a positive and redemptive vision to set against the dead-ends of retributivism and has provided a salutary challenge to entrenched assumptions. However, it may be thought to overstate its case in two major respects: first, its critique of retributivism is not dependent upon a wholly negative view of 'state justice' (as the incorporation of restorative measures into existing penal systems has demonstrated). It may be true that the modern state, in this as in other areas, has tended to act over against civil society rather than as the representative and partner of the communities which it governs, but the intrinsic relation between authorization and enforcement of law, or between the legislative and judicial functions of government, must not be overlooked. Criminal law carries authority as the expression of the will of the political community for the ordering of social relationships, just as law in the Old Testament is the practical expression of the divine will, and the task of doing justice in response to violations is a public rather than a private responsibility. Nevertheless, the paradigm of 'community justice' rightly challenges the state to undertake this task with full regard for the specific effects of crime upon people and relationships, and by means which reinforce rather than diminish the involvement of all citizens in seeking justice as part of the common good.

Second, it may be questioned whether retribution can be sidelined quite as easily as advocates of the restorative model sometimes imply. There are doubts both at the theological and the practical levels. Restoration is certainly the primary aim of God's dealings with sinners in the biblical story, in both Testaments. 'I have no pleasure in the death of anyone, says the Lord GOD; so turn, and live' (Ezekiel 18.32, NRSV, in the context of a divine reply to complaints that 'the way of the

LORD is not just'). 'God sent the Son into the world, not to condemn the world, but that the world might be saved through him' (John 3.17). Christopher Marshall concludes his survey of divine and human punishment in the New Testament with the claim that 'the purpose of this punishment is ultimately reparative or redemptive in design. It is intended to invite repentance and reformation from wrongdoers and/or to frustrate oppressors who seek to repress the gospel or persecute the weak'[12] – a reminder of the educative and disciplinary aspects of punishment which biblical authors attribute to God, but perhaps a selective vision of the tragic aspects of humanity's broken relationship with its Creator.

For the promise of salvation involves both the potential destructiveness of human wrongdoing and wilfulness, and the necessity of choosing life rather than death. Both the divine covenant with humanity and the ordering of society have to reckon with the sombre reality of weakness, perversity and failure. That, after all, is what necessitates systems of criminal justice. The appeal to *ultimate* divine purpose has to reckon also with penultimate factors, and the government of human societies must deal with unintended or unforeseen consequences and not merely the *design* of policies. There is a tendency among those who commend restorative justice to overlook the limits of its applicability and effectiveness in situations of injury and conflict, and to underestimate the ethical and spiritual preconditions of being able to advance beyond retribution. Above all, there is a tendency to evade the dependence of restorative procedures upon a framework of law and coercion, because the administration of justice requires the assertion of authority and the exercise of power against wrongdoing. The words of William Temple deserve to be pondered: 'The most fundamental requirement of any political or economic system is not that it shall express love, though that is desirable, nor that it shall express justice, though that is the first ethical demand to be made upon it, but that it shall supply some reasonable measure of security against murder, robbery and starvation'.[13] We may hope that the enactment and enforcement of law will restrain evil and promote good, but it cannot guarantee a just, harmonious or peaceful outcome, nor can it compel the right use of human freedom.

The confrontation between 'realist' and 'idealist' assumptions about criminal justice raises profound methodological questions about the movement from theological to practical models of justice. While Luther's separation between the Gospel and general social practice is clearly unsatisfactory, it may equally be a mistake to construct a tightly unified theory of justice which fails to respect the distinction between human justice and divine, or between the basic requirements of imperfect human societies and the transcendent demands of divine righteousness. Christians can neither aim to replace the criminal law with the Gospel nor regard the justice of the Gospel as irrelevant to the operation of criminal law.

I have already noted the need to move from 'abstract' to 'embodied' notions of justice. In a trenchant sermon, Bob Hardy provided a vital link by pointing to the vision of the Christian community as 'a flagship, a guiding light for the common life of human beings'.[14] It may provide a model for society by challenging prevalent assumptions about human goods and demonstrating the possibility of creative transformation. Much of what has been recovered in contemporary practices of restorative justice has its roots in the Church's system of penitential discipline, as both Oliver O'Donovan[15] and Duncan Forrester[16] have pointed out (while nevertheless drawing different implications for our understanding of punishment in society). We ought to recognize the difference between the functions of the Church and the state, and the resources available to each respectively, while expecting the Church to commend ways of dealing with wrongdoing in society which move towards, rather than away from, the justice which is revealed in the Gospel.

Hardy's appeal to the embodiment of justice in a common life rests on the insight of Richard Hooker that 'Justice is the virtue whereby that good which wanteth in ourselves we receive at the hands of others'.[17] He goes on to comment,

> Justice is the virtue of a society whose members are committed to constructive engagement with one another. Justice is the virtue of mutual trust and mutual gift. It's what happens when commitment is realised and people are valued: 'as they are sociable parts united into one body – a law which bindeth them each to serve unto others' good;', to quote Hooker once more.[18]

This may be contrasted with the relatively 'thin' concept of justice as treatment according to desert, with its atomized and individualized portrayal of human action and human good, its failure to explore the social context in which wrongs are committed and goods are pursued, its insensitivity to the significance of human interdependence, for good and for ill – and, might one add, its bland confidence in our ability to make far-reaching judgements about the deserts of our fellow human beings?

Two major consequences may be adduced. First, if justice is a social virtue expressive of our dependence upon one another to realize the good which we lack in ourselves, criminal justice must be set in the wider context of social justice. An individualized approach to crime and punishment, which belongs naturally with the individualization of redemptive grace, obscures the responsibility of society as a whole, and particularly that of the powerful and the successful, for maintaining or countering the social, economic and cultural forces which foster criminal activity and attitudes. First-hand acquaintance with the criminal justice system confirms W. H. Auden's depressing but challenging insight that 'Those to whom evil is done/Do evil in return.'[19] Would that the zeal of politicians and saloon bar pundits for being 'tough on crime' were matched by informed and persistent toughness on the causes of crime. The righteousness of which the Hebrew Scriptures speak embraces the public domain as much as the family circle, and makes demands upon the Treasury as well as the Home Office. It holds before us the truth that the problems and failings of parts of society are the problems and failings of the whole and must be accepted as such (another application of the Pauline metaphor of the body to the life of society). If this is so, there can be no question of regarding the law-abiding and the transgressors of the law as different species, and however much the public needs to be protected from a small minority of highly dangerous offenders, no solution to the problem of crime can be sought purely in terms of stigmatizing, incapacitating or excluding an 'underclass' from participation in society.

Second and following, if justice 'bindeth us to serve unto others' good', it calls for qualities of patience, imagination and generosity in dealing with violations of the law and peace of the community. Justice conceived as 'putting right' may require giving certain people *more* than their deserts viewed narrowly, for the sake of the future and the common good. It requires not only a 'new deal' for victims of crime, but a refusal to place offenders beyond the pale. The long-term aim of the criminal justice system must in most cases be the reintegration of the offender into society, and to that end it is imperative that the necessarily retributive aspect of doing justice must at least not impede, and preferably serve, the complementary aim of restoration. The Gospel provides us with the vision of human potential and the self-knowledge which are necessary to nurture and cherish this understanding of justice. A sixteenth-century observer, seeing a group of prisoners being led off to execution said, 'There, but for the grace of God, goes John Bradford.' A society which rejects the claims of mercy and the need for hope, and forgets their roots in compassion and humility, is not only morally deficient but practically impeded in its response to crime. Conversely, the working out of this vision of justice requires co-operation between professionals in the criminal justice system and voluntary groups who share their concerns. Seeking justice in society is an important goal both of Christian discipleship and active citizenship.

To sum up: I have suggested that, rather than being identified with justice understood as retribution, the institution of state punishment must be viewed in relation to justice as a norm defining the overall goals of social policy. The shift in terminology from 'penal system' to 'criminal justice system' is a significant acknowledgement of changing orientations and priorities. The failure of Christian theology to inform and criticize the operation of systems of criminal justice has been attributed in some measure to the division between Law and Gospel at the time of the Reformation, and an over-individualized view of the redemptive grace of God. I have attempted to sketch the major elements of biblical thinking about justice and righteousness, emphasizing the creative and formative character of divine justice, and its embodiment for redemptive and restorative purposes in the history of Jesus Christ. However, while a restorative perspective on justice corrects the defects of a retributive perspective, I claim that it cannot entirely displace it, because it underestimates the moral and social significance of law and evades the role of coercion in the administration of justice.

Finally, I have expressed reservations about the validity of moving too directly from models of divine justice to systems of human justice, but I have suggested that – in preference to more abstract definitions – the embodiment of justice in the common life of a covenant community provides a salutary model of human interaction and mutual responsibility. This enables us to avoid both a complacent conservatism and an unrealistic perfectionism in our assessment of the institution of state punishment. The effect of such a model is to challenge the individualistic assumptions of a retributive penal policy and to suggest that a society's response to crime cannot be conveyed by penal measures alone but must be expressed in a sense of responsibility for promoting healthy and inclusive relationships between its members, including trustful and constructive engagement with those who have offended against its laws.

It may be asked whether a vision of society which is rooted in the particularities of Christian belief and practice can be publicly accessible, or whether it must remain a sectarian possession. A theology which regards the social responsibility of the churches as integral rather than peripheral must emphatically reply, 'No', and one major reason for this is the character of justice as embodied rather than abstract. It was Hooker's view that the inheritance of Christianity is not a set of doctrines, but a way of life which can be offered to the judgement of the whole world for testing and evaluation. If that is the case, Christians involved with criminal justice issues will find many allies and collaborators as they discover common ground in shared engagement with the concrete problems and opportunities of seeking justice in an unjust world. In such a setting the Christian contribution has a firm centre in the love and mercy and righteousness of God, but its boundaries will be limited only by the extent of the Church's participation in the life of the world. The challenges and opportunities before members of the churches and those who speak and act for them publicly are unlikely to diminish as the practical and ethical dilemmas of responding to crime demand continual attention to the meaning of justice as a divine gift and a human goal.

Notes

1 A classic example is H. B. Acton (ed.), *The Philosophy of Punishment.* Macmillan, London, 1969.
2 Hardy, Robert, Oxford University Sermon (unpublished), preached at Lincoln College, Oxford, 3 November 1996, p. 1.
3 On this, see further James D. G. Dunn and Alan M. Suggate, *The Justice of God* (Part 1). Paternoster Press, Carlisle, 1993.
4 Luther, Martin, 'Autobiographical Fragment', March 1545, reprinted in

E. G. Rupp and Benjamin Drewery (eds), *Martin Luther*, Documents of Modern History series. Edward Arnold, London, 1970, p. 6.

5 Calvin, John, *Institutes of the Christian Religion* (1559 edition), II.xvi.1.

6 Calvin, *Institutes*, II.xvi.2.

7 Gorringe, Timothy, *God's Just Vengeance*. CUP, Cambridge, 1996, pp. 1–5.

8 Snyder, T. Richard, *The Protestant Ethic and the Spirit of Punishment*. Eerdmans, Grand Rapids/Cambridge, 2001, esp. ch. 3.

9 Zehr, Howard, *Changing Lenses: A New Focus for Crime and Justice*. Herald Press, Scottdale, PA, 1990.

10 Marshall, Christopher D., *Beyond Retribution: A New Testament Vision for Justice, Crime and Punishment*. Eerdmans, Grand Rapids/Cambridge, 2001.

11 Zehr, *Changing Lenses*, ch. 10.

12 Marshall, *Beyond Retribution*, pp. 198–9.

13 Temple, William, *Christianity and Social Order*. Shepheard-Walwyn/SPCK, London, 1976, p. 61.

14 Hardy, University Sermon, p. 2.

15 O'Donovan, Oliver, *The Desire of the Nations: Rediscovering the Roots of Political Theology*. CUP, Cambridge, 1996, pp. 146–51.

16 Forrester, Duncan B., *Christian Justice and Public Policy*. CUP, Cambridge, 1997, pp. 78–80.

17 Hooker, Richard, *A Learned Sermon Of the Nature of Pride*, II.

18 Hardy, University Sermon, p. 2.

19 Auden, W. H., 'September 1, 1939'.

5 | Making the Punishment Fit the Needs of Society: The Constructive Role of Prisons

Harry Woolf

I T IS NOW NEARLY 12 YEARS since, on 1 April 1990, the first and most serious of six prison disturbances occurred at Manchester Strangeways Prison. The disturbances resulted in my being asked to conduct an inquiry, the second part of which was undertaken together with Judge Stephen Tumim.

It was the Strangeways Inquiry which brought me in contact with the Right Reverend Robert Hardy, who had already been Bishop to Her Majesty's Prisons for five years and was to continue to hold that office for more than a further ten years. In the course of conducting the inquiry, I received most valuable advice from the Bishop and I am delighted to have the opportunity of acknowledging his personal achievements in improving the conditions in our prisons by making this modest contribution for this publication in his honour.

Before the disturbance broke out in Strangeways, the prison, which was the largest in this country and one of the largest in Europe, had many handicaps to overcome. It was overcrowded and had a very mixed population of prisoners. While there had been an improvement in some of the living conditions, the conditions were still mainly insanitary and degrading. Prisoners were spending far too long in their cells and there were frequent problems about clothing, prisoners having to go without socks or having to wear ill-fitting secondhand shoes. It was often impossible to provide prisoners with clean towels.

The prison did, however, have, as I reported, one area 'where the prison was flourishing'. This was in relation to its religious activities. For this the Reverend Noel Proctor, senior Church of England chaplain, was entitled to claim a substantial part of the credit. His services in the chapel were regularly attended by between 300 and 400 prisoners. However, it was in the chapel on a Sunday when the service was being conducted by Mr Proctor that the riot started which ignited the other disturbances.

At the time I recognized that the level of attendance at services could, in part, have resulted from the lack of alternative activities at Strangeways. However, it was clear that religion was playing an important part in the lives of many inmates and that Mr Proctor and his colleagues were a hugely positive influence on the prison.

Since those times I have visited many other prisons and invariably I have found a similar contribution being made by chaplains. In my meetings with the then Bishop for Prisons and many members of the Chaplaincy, I have been conscious that the chaplains are a significant force for good within the prison system. In the time which has elapsed since Strangeways, their task has not grown any easier. The prison population has increased by over 50 per cent but the percentage of inmates who contend they have 'no religion' has grown by a much greater percentage, 101 per cent, over the same period. Furthermore, most of the prisoners who fall within this category are young prisoners serving relatively short sentences. They are the type of prisoner likely to re-offend when they are released unless something can be done to change their attitudes.

Young offenders are at the heart of the problems experienced by the Prison Service. They contribute to overcrowding. Their impact on criminal justice statistics helps explain why it is so difficult to achieve a situation where the criminal justice system makes a real contribution to the whole of society.

Conducting the Strangeways Inquiry made me aware of just how important the way we treat our prisoners is for the whole of society. I was left in no doubt that this country could not have an effective criminal justice system unless it had a prison system which was just and humane and tackled offending behaviour of inmates. That was not the position at that time and, alas, it is still not the position today.

Past neglect means there is a lot of ground to make up, but I am confident that, if the Prison Service received the support that it deserved, this country could have a prison system of which it could be proud.

The importance of this was recognized by Winston Churchill in 1910: 'the mood and tenor of a nation can be judged by the way it treats its criminals and there's treasure in the heart of every man if only you can find it'.

Although 11 years have passed since my report, I do not believe that any objective commentator would suggest that this country has as effective a prison system as it should have. However, I do not believe that the fault lies with those who work within our prisons, and certainly it does not lie with the Chaplaincy. With very few exceptions, those who gave evidence at the Inquiry and who I have met, impressed me as being deeply committed to achieving the objectives of the Prison Service expressed in the Prison Service Statement of Purpose which provides, 'Her Majesty's Prison Service serves the public by keeping in custody those committed by the courts. Our duty is to look after them with humanity and help them lead law-abiding and useful lives in custody and after release.'

At the present time, great emphasis is being placed by the government on improving public services. But the poor relation, so far as additional resources are concerned, is likely to remain the Prison Service. Just consider the difficulties it faces:

- it has no control over the number of inmates it has to keep safely in custody;
- it cannot impose any minimum standards of eligibility for a prison career so its customers have a remarkable range of talents – few of them attractive;
- it deals with customers who have not chosen to be there and would positively like to be elsewhere;
- it fulfils different roles for its different customers. For some that role involves being no more than a turnkey, but others need a teacher or a medical carer. The Prison Service also runs mother-and-baby units and old-age homes.

Sir David Ramsbotham, the last Chief Inspector of Prisons, was quoted as saying that if you stripped out of the prison population the kids, the elderly and the mentally ill, the asylum-seekers and those who have committed minor offences, the population would be reduced by 20,000 from a whole-time high of 67,000, and rising.

Here are a few of the worrying statistics:

- more than two out of three prisoners are unemployed when they enter prison (14 times the current unemployment rate);
- one in three prisoners has been homeless at some time;
- around half of sentenced prisoners are reported to have run away from home as children;
- around half of prisoners have used drugs in the year prior to being imprisoned;
- half of all prisoners screened on reception are at or below level 1 in reading, two-thirds in numeracy and four-fifths in writing (Level 1 is what is expected from an 11-year-old);
- nine out of ten young offenders have mental health problems.

My title is meant to make a point. It is based on Gilbert and Sullivan's delightful song in which the Mikado argues that the punishment must fit the crime. It is suggested that this would be 'an object all sublime'. With this I agree, but punishment is only part of the court's objective when it imposes imprisonment on someone who has been found guilty of a crime. The punishment is not intended to be confined to retribution and deterrence but is intended to do more. It is intended to meet all the conflicting expectations of the punishment imposed by the state. What are these expectations other than that those who commit crimes should be justly punished? It is that the punishment should protect the public by reducing crime, and in particular violent crime, and that it should rehabilitate the offender by making it less likely that the offender will offend again. In other words, it should cut the cycle of offending, imprisonment, release and further offending.

If these aims could be achieved it could restore, maintain and enhance the public's confidence in the criminal justice system. In the case of imprisonment, that includes making the statement that 'prison is an expensive way of making people worse' obsolete.

There was a time when I thought that a worse outcome was more likely than not to be the result of a prison sentence. Prison remains expensive – very expensive. But I now believe that it can be an expensive way of making people better. This does not mean that I want to see more people going to prison or spending longer in prison then they do now. On the contrary, I think it is essential that we should send fewer people to prison and should in general send them to prison for shorter periods. Prison should be and should remain the last resort.

Whenever a person is sentenced to imprisonment, the sentence should be for the shortest period that is possible in all the circumstances. This would enable the Prison Service, as it should, to focus on the long-term prisoners in their custody since, as John Halliday has pointed out, very little can be achieved during short sentences. The Halliday Report is one signpost to a better future. Another is the Sentencing Advisory Panel, and a third is the Youth Justice Board.

The conflicting expectations as to what can be achieved by punishment create a real dilemma for the Prison Service. The fact that prison is meant to be a punishment makes it more difficult for the Prison Service to tackle a prisoner's offending behaviour. The courts do not send prisoners to prison *for* punishment, but *as a* punishment. Imprisonment is a punishment because the prisoner loses the control over those activities which the ordinary member of the public enjoys. This creates a tension with achieving rehabilitation, since tackling offending behaviour involves the offender recognizing that you have a choice and taking responsibility for making the right choice.

Unfortunately, unless a sentence is for a fairly substantial period, prisoners never begin to tackle their offending behaviour. While I accept that positive things can be and are done in prison, they can be done more effectively and more economically in the community. That is why, if there is an option of imposing a community sentence or a prison sentence, a community sentence should always be imposed. Initiatives such as curfews and tagging can make a real contribution here.

Today, too few community sentences are imposed and too many and too long prison sentences are imposed. The consequences are doubly destructive of the needs of society. It means that the best opportunity of tackling an offender's offending behaviour is lost.

Why should there be too few community sentences? There are a number of reasons, but at the forefront is the regrettable fact that neither the public nor sentencers have sufficient confidence in the community alternative. This absence of confidence is usually unjustified and is the product of a lack of information – a lack which can and should be tackled. The reality as to what prison can and cannot achieve needs repeating again and again and again. We need to show by independent research what can be achieved in the community and what cannot.

I hope a contribution towards this end will be made by an imaginative initiative about to be launched by the Prison Reform Trust with funding by the Fairbairn Foundation. PRT are going to discuss with sentencers at all levels, from Recorder to High Court Judge, actual cases on the borderline for a custodial sentence. The aim is to find out why sentencers feel compelled to choose the prison option. In this way it is hoped to identify what would be required to enable them to choose the non-custodial option. Pragmatic research of this nature may enable us to improve the acceptability of punishment in the community. In addition we need to establish more imaginative community punishments. Without committing myself to the detail (and the devil is always in the detail), this is why I warmly welcome the Home Secretary's recent announcement of a third way, including weekend prisons. If we can find the third way then the Prison Service will be able to tackle in a wholly different manner the offending behaviour of serious criminals; the criminals with which only the Prison Service can deal.

I have repeatedly made the point that the biggest challenge facing the Prison Service is overcrowding. Since I became Lord Chief Justice two years ago, I have naturally been conscious of my responsibilities to provide leadership as to the correct approach to sentencing – a sense of responsibility which the Director General, Martin Narey, underlined by providing me with compelling statistics to demonstrate how even reducing all sentences by a few months would make a real but modest contribution to reducing overcrowding.

However, I have become acutely conscious that within our existing structures there is little the judiciary can themselves achieve. Guideline judgements can help to achieve greater consistency. The Sentencing Advisory Panel does provide the most valuable information for achieving better sentencing, but greater changes are necessary which will not be provided by attacking the present sentencing policy. For example, the Panel is to carry out research as to the cost of individual sentences. If the public were aware of the cost of our present policies they might become less complacent.

At the present time, to reduce sentences for violent crime would be to undermine further the public's confidence in the criminal justice system. For offences of dishonesty, which do not involve violence, I believe that the courts do not now usually impose prison sentences unless they believe there is no alternative.

I am of course aware that my judgement as to offences involving mobile phones has been largely regarded as increasing sentences for mobile telephone muggers. I do not regret the extensive publicity that the judgement received. The publicity means that both the public and muggers will be under no illusion as to the stand which the courts are taking on this class of offence. However, at the beginning of the judgement of the court, I made it clear that I was not setting out new guidelines; rather I was reaffirming the effect of the existing sentencing policy the courts have been adopting for some time. Rightly, in my judgement, the courts have been imposing deterrent sentences to tackle prevalent offences. The great majority of the public felt they were in need of protection against these offences, the victims of which were all too often vulnerable members of the community. The courts have a responsibility to make their contribution to tackling the serious problem that these offences are creating. The courts have been meeting that responsibility and I hope that my judgement had the effect of making those who are tempted to commit these offences aware of what the price will be if they are brought to justice.

It is no use imposing deterrent sentences if those who should be deterred are unaware of how the courts are responding to these offences. I have no doubt that the courts have a responsibility to assist in resolving this problem.

As it happens, on the very same day that my judgement in relation to telephone mugging was published, *The Times* reported a case which sent out a different message. It was my judgement in a case involving a woman with two children, who had not previously been before the courts. The offences were two in number and involved filling in forms dishonestly in order to obtain credit. The amount of credit eventually obtained was substantial. However, the woman had been in real need and had done her best to repay her indebtedness. We said that to send her to prison for eight months was wrong in principle and we stated that sending her to prison would result in harm to the children, of whom she was the sole carer. We emphasized, and in this respect the case may have broken new ground, that it was good sentencing practice to take into account the explosion which there has been in the female prison population. We set out the statistics and gave a clear steer about the need to avoid sending a person to prison in those circumstances. We added that if it had been necessary to send her to prison, a sentence of one month's imprisonment would achieve exactly the same objectives as the sentence of eight months.

The distinction between the two situations is that to impose a non-custodial sentence in the case of the offence of dishonesty would not undermine the public's confidence in the criminal justice system. It is for the judiciary to impose the sentences which they consider are just, and the public cannot dictate what sentence is appropriate in particular cases. However, it is a responsibility of the judiciary to take into account the needs of society as a whole and the victims of a crime in particular when establishing guidelines as what punishment suits a particular category of crime.

Turning to the second part of the Statement of Purpose, dealing with the manner in which the Prison Service should look after those who the courts commit into its custody, I would lay particular stress on the need to 'help them lead law abiding and useful lives in custody and *after release*'. Since I became Lord Chief Justice I have had an insight into the work which the members of the Prison Service perform in preparing reports to assist those who have responsibility for determining whether lifers who have completed the tariff part of the sentence are ready to be released on licence. The same is true in relation to the reviews which I am required to make as an interim measure in the case of young offenders detained during Her Majesty's Pleasure. I find that the reports of prison staff are prepared with immense care and that they are a great help. The reports also make clear the quality of work which is taking place to prepare for the return of these young offenders to the community. Of course it is inevitable that on occasions mistakes will be made, but fortunately, thanks in part to the work done by the members of the Prison Service, the mistakes are rare.

The Prison Service is managing to handle those youngsters who have committed the most serious offences, and so constitute the gravest risks for the future, extremely well. As you read the successive reports, a picture emerges of young offenders who are not only maturing, but whose attitudes, values and behaviour are being transformed. This enables me to reduce their tariffs in many cases.

The judiciary make a significant contribution to the work of the Parole Board. However, apart from the work with lifers and their contribution to the Parole Board, the judiciary's involvement with those whom they have sentenced ceases with the conclusion of the court proceedings. A change which I hope we will see in the future is a continued involvement between the sentencer and the sentenced. The introduction of IT should enable the judiciary at least to receive feedback as to the progress a prisoner makes during a sentence. But more is needed. I would like to see the judiciary having a continued responsibility for a prisoner until he or she is returned to the community. If and when the necessary resources (including IT) become available, I would like sentencing judges to retain responsibility for monitoring prisoners' progress. In this way judges could make suggestions as to the steps prisoners should take to equip themselves to become law-abiding citizens on their return to the community and, if their progress justifies this, authorize their early release on licence. This could provide a real incentive to prisoners to strive to improve themselves while in prison. It could reduce the likelihood of them re-offending and again becoming numbers in the prison population. It would also be very salutary for the judiciary, who will learn what sentences work.

While it is always necessary to be careful to ensure that initiatives do not have unintended consequences, more flexibility as to the manner in which a sentence is served must be desirable. In my report after Strangeways, I commended the community prison as a way of reducing those consequences. But the rise in the prison population made this a pipe-dream.

I read with great interest Stephen Pryor's paper *The Responsible Prisoner* (Home Office 2001). He is undoubtedly right when he says that imprisonment inevitably results in some loss of responsibility on the part of a prisoner and that the Prison Service should seek to ensure that that loss is kept to a minimum. More importantly, he is right to emphasize the need for the Prison Service to ensure that at the end of a sentence 'the prisoner can once again take up the responsibilities of free citizenship'. If it fails in doing this, it not only fails the prisoner, but fails the public it is paid to protect.

I do not believe that the Prison Service can achieve this last responsibility by itself: it needs the help of the other agencies. These agencies can ensure that ex-prisoners receive the help they need after release from prison to ensure that they can properly take responsibility for themselves. The truly depressing figures as to re-offending and reconviction rates of those released from prison underline the need for this. The Prison Service cannot control the behaviour of an offender once the offender has left prison.

The Prison Service can and must do what is within its power to ensure that the necessary support is in place in the community when the prisoner is released. There need to be more effective links than there are at present between the Prison Service, the Probation Service and the other agencies who have to take the primary responsibility as to what happens to released prisoners. Again, this important role of the Prison Service would be facilitated by the ability of a community prison to foster closer links with the community to which the prisoner is to return.

Society needs punishments which will reduce offending. Most objective onlookers recognize the limits of what can be achieved by deterrence and retribution alone. We have to focus more than we have in the past on rehabilitation. Punishment has not only to fit the crime but also must meet the needs of society. Given the right resources, the voluntary sector could achieve wonders by the provision of education and training in prisons. This is what is likely to increase a prisoner's sense of responsibility, and with increased responsibility will come a reduction in re-offending. Human rights is all about human dignity. Prisoners are entitled to retain their dignity. To do so they must be treated with decency, and the courts and the other agencies involved in the criminal justice system must help the Prison Service in its efforts to ensure that it meets its own Statement of Purpose.

This could be a critical time, a turning point, for prisons. The cancer from which the Prison Service has been continually suffering – overcrowding – could be conquered. The Prison Service could be a constructive force within society, playing its full part in a just and effective criminal justice system supporting and supported by the courts and the Probation Service. This is a truly 'sublime' prospect of which the Mikado would have been proud.

6 | Shades of the Prison House?

David Ramsbotham

> Shades of the prison house begin to close
> Upon the growing boy,
> But he beholds the light and whence it flows . . .
> At length the man perceives it die away
> And fade into the light of common day.
>
> William Wordsworth, 'Ode on the Intimations of Immortality'

It may seem strange to begin a chapter of a book with the word 'future' in its title, with well-known lines that could be taken as being backward looking. But I choose them deliberately to make the point that, in order to look forward, one must first look back, to remind oneself of how it is that a present situation has come to pass.

When I first became acquainted with the Criminal Justice System in this country, on taking up the appointment of Her Majesty's Chief Inspector of Prisons in December 1995, I was very surprised to find that it was not a system at all. It seemed to consist of a number of individual warring tribes, all competing with each other for diminishing resources. Courts, police, prisons and probation did not make it their practice to consider their impact on any other component part; neither politicians nor officials seemed to consider the impact of one piece of legislation, such as putting more police officers on the streets or demanding more severe sentencing of particular groups of offenders, on either the Prison or Probation Services. Certainly the Treasury, in its relentless search for savings, did not consider the impact on prisons of cuts in their funding. Having spent a lifetime in the Army, where much of our time was taken up with ensuring that people worked together, without which co-operation nothing effective could happen, I was staggered to find such opposite practice in other operational services.

Why was this, and how had it come to pass? Up until about 150 years ago, sentencers had three options open to them – hanging, transportation and imprisonment. Prisons were mainly used to house those awaiting trial, those awarded short sentences and those sentenced for debt. But when transportation ended, more and more people ended up in prison, which prompted a development that is at the base of all our troubles today – because it was not properly thought through.

By 1877 there were two entirely different prison systems in the country. Local prisons (paid for by local taxes), the old gaols, bridewells, houses of correction and penitentiaries, held all those not yet sentenced and those serving short sentences. These were supplemented by what were referred to as 'modern' prisons, beginning with Pentonville in 1842, built in many inner-city areas, and, after the end of transportation, called convict prisons, holding those serving longer sentences.

With shades of today, these two were nationalized under a Prison Commission, allegedly in order to save money by cutting out one line of management, and relieving the local tax burden, particularly on rural areas, at a time of agricultural depression. But in fact, the merger created a fault-line that has bedevilled the organization and conduct of imprisonment ever since. Essentially local prisons held those who were unsentenced, presumed innocent in the eyes of the law until proven guilty, and convict prisons held those who had been awarded a sentence period of deprivation of liberty – their punishment for their crime. Each group has different needs that should be reflected in both the conditions in which they are held and the treatment that they receive.

In other words, far from making things easier for those who were responsible and accountable for the treatment of and conditions for prisoners, administrative convenience was seen as being a more important end in itself by those working in Whitehall Ministries. That fault-line has not been mended to this day, and remains the main cause of many of today's problems. This is an issue that can and must be tackled if the future of our prisons is to be better than its present and its past.

Thankfully, one of the first actions of New Labour when it came to power in 1997 was to issue a single aim to the whole of the Criminal Justice System that could not be clearer or easier to understand. Put very simply, it is to 'Protect the public by preventing crime'.

It could be said that prisons should concentrate on preventing 're-crime', because people would not be in prison unless they had committed, or been accused of committing, a crime. But what it means is preventing the next crime, or, as the motto of Lancaster Farms Young Offender's Institution has it, 'Prevent the next victim'. This fits in well with the Statement of Purpose of the Prison Service, written in 1983, and not bettered by anything that I have seen:

> Her Majesty's Prison Service serves the public by keeping in custody those committed by the courts. Our duty is to look after them with humanity and help them lead law-abiding and useful lives in custody and on release.

There are, in fact, two parts to this Purpose. One talks about security and humanity, the other about resettlement, and it is a pity that politicians always seem to concentrate on the former. Their approach was typified in the vast expenditure on improvement to physical security after the 1994–5 escapes from Whitemoor and Parkhurst, and the then Home Secretary Michael Howard's pejorative cry for concentration on 'security, security, security'. Recently, the European Convention of Human Rights became the law of the land. There was considerable panic about the implications of this, which there need not have been if people had compared them with Prison Rules. There is no difference between them, and so a breach of one is a breach of the other. The fact that so many Rules had been broken or ignored in the past is what needs to be corrected, because they have been broken – not because they now equate to a breach of Human Rights, likely to lead to expensive litigation.

In fact, the aim is all about helping prisoners to lead law-abiding and useful lives in prison and on release, with the qualifications that they must be held securely and treated with humanity throughout the period of their sentence. In other words, the aim of the Prison Service is to protect the public by preventing re-offending, which is to prevent the next crime.

But by the time that the Statement of Purpose and the Aim were written, the Prison Commission had disappeared, thanks to what I have always regarded as a most uncharacteristic error by the then Home Secretary, 'Rab' Butler. In 1962, distracted by a number of other problems, he failed to give full attention to the implications of the proposal by his then Permanent Secretary that, because prisons took up so much of the Home Office budget, the Prison Commission should be abolished, replaced by a Prison Department under a career civil servant. Now, whatever they are or can do, civil servants are not, and are not trained to be, operational commanders, which is what the Director General of the operational Prison Service actually is. Quite rightly, they see it as their first duty to serve the Minister or Ministers whom they have been appointed to support.

But it is quite wrong to expect governors of prisons, for example, to regard their first duty as being to serve Ministers, any more than it is right for Commanding Officers of Army units. Their first duty is to those for whom they are responsible – staff, prisoners and those who work in prisons. Of course they are accountable to Ministers, for the exercise of their responsibility, but that must be through a managerial structure, designed to protect them from excessive bureaucratic demands.

The Prison Service is now an Agency, on paper as independent as any other 'Next Steps' Agency set up by the previous Conservative administration. In fact they are not independent of the Home Office, which, in addition to providing its budget, maintains a tight hold on many of its doings, including such details as senior appointments. It is the Home Office that approves the myriad of Targets and Performance Indicators that officials love to regard as evidence of the quality of performance, when they are too often nothing of the sort. In sum, the Prison Service is now a confused hybrid – it is run like a Whitehall Ministry, and its vastly inflated Headquarters functions like any other Department. But its operational units, its prisons, while their budgets and their compliance with regulations are monitored in minute detail, do not receive any clear instructions about what they are expected to achieve with the prisoners whom they hold – only that they are not to let them escape.

This state of affairs has been brought about because Ministers and officials have either lost sight of, or have never thought through, what the purpose of imprisonment actually is. And yet the answer is staring them in the face, set out in the Aim that they have laid down for the Criminal Justice System and the supporting Statement of Purpose of the Prison Service.

Prisons are, like hospitals in the National Health Service, the acute part of the CJS, where treatment takes place. Only those who need treatment should be sent there – prisons, like hospitals, have no control over who comes in. Also like hospitals, that treatment will not be completed while the patient or prisoner is in hospital or prison – it will have to be completed in the community in the form of aftercare. There are, of course, other parts to that analogy. Some will prove to be incurable. Some will have to come back for repeat or alternative treatment. It is said that if you stay too long in hospital you risk picking up some bug from the stones. If you stay too long in prison you risk being corrupted by the other prisoners. But as far as prisons within the CJS are concerned, it is important to realize that the imperative fuel of any treatment process is information about the patient or prisoner upon which treatment plans can be based. In the case of prisons, this must come from courts, the police, the Probation Service, the social services, the Health Service and education. Sadly, that is by no means an automatic process, and hours of time are taken in chasing up essential information from those who have it, but do not think of passing it on. My fellow CJS Inspectors studied this and published a joint report in June 2000 making specific recommendations for improvement. So far they have been greeted, like all too many other such reports, with a deafening silence, which again suggests that Ministers and officials are not tuned in to an aim.

Once a prisoner has been received, it is the task of the prison staff to assess both the risk to the public that he or she presents, which will determine the security category of the prison in which they well be held, and the various needs that have contributed to the offending or anti-social behaviour that led to the punished crime. This is poorly done at present, shallow assessments and patchy procedures contributing to many shoddy assessments.

Unfortunately, risk is seen more as risk of embarrassing Ministers, or the reputation of the Prison Service, than risk to the public. I will return to this later because I believe that this could be turned to advantage if that embarrassment could be focused on the achievement of the aim of protecting the public by preventing crime.

I suggest that there are five needs that must be assessed, in addition to offending and anti-social behaviour problems. First, of course, must come education. I will not repeat all the hideous statistics of how many have a reading age of less than eight, how many have excluded themselves or been evicted from school or how many have no educational qualifications of any kind. Many of these result from undiagnosed learning difficulties of various kinds, including dyslexia. But I believe that everyone, on first coming into prison, must be put through a standard educational needs assessment, which moves with a prisoner wherever they go within the system. It does not need to be repeated – I found one prisoner who had been put through nine separate assessments, but had taken part in no consequent education – which is not to say that it could not be updated to record achievement. Unfortunately the Prison Service has wasted countless available hours of education time that could have been devoted to basic education for those who were in dire need of it, because it set itself a target of school leaving age education, based on a wrong interpretation of figures. That too would not have happened had there been a proper aim for all prisons.

The second assessment must be of job skills and job potential. It is said that the three things most likely to prevent re-offending are a home, a job and a stable relationship. All three are put at risk by imprisonment, to which the Prison Service contributes by keeping far too many prisoners locked up all day doing nothing. I believe that everyone should be put through a simple aptitude test, which will give an indication of potential. Work training must be related not just to this potential but to the possibility of employment in the area to which the prisoner will return. I would add one other rider to this. While in the Army, I became involved with a scheme to which I was alerted by one of my staff. Aptitude tests can indicate a person's potential to fill certain jobs. If jobs were described in such a way that individual aptitude could be assessed and presented as a potential, which could then be confirmed by interview, no names need be given, and ex-offenders could compete on equal terms, at least until the interview stage.

The third assessment must be of social skills, the ability to live a useful as well as a law-abiding life in the community. This must concentrate, for example, on prisoners' ability to look after themselves, or, as one course has it, 'to learn to live alone', including how to cope with the bureaucracy of the welfare state. In this connection can come vocational training skills such as painting and decorating, as well as domestic skills such as cooking. Parenting skills are woefully absent from many who are already parents.

The fourth is health, both physical and mental, highlighted by the admirable report produced by the Office of National Statistics in 1998, which showed that 70 per cent of all prisoners were suffering from some form of identifiable personality disorder, which went up to 90 per cent if the effects of substance abuse were added. This does not say that all prisoners are sectionable under the Mental Health Act, but that they have a problem that inhibits their ability to live useful and law-abiding lives in prison and on release, which must be identified. Learning difficulties and other problems must be identified early so that prisoners are not faced with demands with which they cannot cope.

In addition to being wells of psychiatric morbidity, prisons are also considerable sources of public health problems. Inevitably those who have been involved with drugs are prey to the blood-transmitted viruses such as HIV and Hepatitis C. Those who have lived rough, or come from other countries, are increasingly found to have TB. Virtually none know how to look after themselves, and are distinctly unfit, which can have an impact on job prospects. So full physical and mental health assessments are a must.

Linked to the concern that prisons are a public health issue, I was amazed to find that the Prison Service was not part of the NHS. Prisoners came from the NHS and would return to it after sentence, so why were they not part of it while serving their sentence? They should not leave it while they were unsentenced, which they appeared to do, because their liberty and citizen's rights had not been affected by the sentence of a court. Five years after publishing a discussion document 'Patient or Prisoner?', in which I advocated that the NHS should assume responsibility for primary, secondary and mental health care in prisons, a Task Force is currently trying to bring this about by making each prison contract for these services from its local provider. But it is ever so slow! Meanwhile, the Prison Service does not deliver the equivalence of treatment that it claims, nor satisfy its public health responsibility.

The final need to be assessed is substance abuse. At least 60 per cent of those received into prison are abusing at the time of reception, and yet, still, compulsory testing is not the norm. I would make it so, and, as at HMP Altcourse for example, separate those who test positive from those who test negative from that moment on. Those who test negative can be subjected to random, voluntary testing, as a condition of their remaining on 'drug-free' wings. The others should be further tested to determine what treatment needs they have – is it detoxification followed by courses according to the severity of their addiction, or is it something of lower level including education, which suggests that they can be put on to 'drug-free' wings on probation?

The misery that I saw caused by the bullying and intimidation practised by drug dealers in prison has helped to convince me that the time has come to accept that a new approach is needed, even to the extent of considering legalization or prescription. As with alcohol in America, prohibition simply does not work, as the vast amounts of money made by criminals proves. Legal purchase of drugs should be linked to extensive education and treatment programmes in the community, starting at an early age. An American Army friend of mine, General Barry McCaffrey, was made the US drug czar by President Clinton. He coined the motto, 'Prevent tomorrow's market.'

Action should be taken against the dealers, spearheaded by the removal of their illegal market which, in heroin alone, amounts to some £4.5 billion per year, the 2,175,000 users being responsible for 20 per cent of the crime in the country. Prohibition does not work, and so a far more radical approach, however unthinkable at present, is needed, such as decriminalization or legalization. Of course there are risks, but who wants the present misery to remain?

Now all this may seem very well known, and readers may be wondering why I am repeating it in a chapter about the future. The answer is that although the aim is clear, and the required measures are obvious, neither is being implemented. Ministers appear to be embarrassed only by the escape of a high-risk prisoner. I wish that they felt equally embarrassed by the failure of the Prison Service to prevent 55 per cent of adults and 80 per cent of young offenders from re-offending within two years of release, because, if they did, they would be forced to ask the currently unasked question – why?

There are two other factors connected with this deplorable situation that I find equally extraordinary.

First, the Prison Service saddles itself with a myriad of targets and performance indicators, few of which have any relevance to the aim, and none of which are to do with resettlement. I would have thought that Ministers would have made this the prime requirement so that they are aware of what is or is not working, and what resources are required to ensure that there is an improvement in their protection of their electorate. But no; this data is not collected, in favour of a mass of meaningless figures all to do with process and none to do with outcomes.

It would be a very simple step for the Home Secretary to order such data to be collected, stating that it must list every prison and record every intervention with a prisoner, to record both negative as well as positive information. It is small wonder that so many re-offend when so many spend most of every day locked up in their cells doing nothing. Hopefully, naming and shaming will end this practice, and force prisons to concentrate on helping prisoners to live useful and law-abiding lives.

Second is the fact that many ways of achieving the aim have been pointed out in official reports, including those of the Inspectorate of Prisons, over a number of years. I find it totally inexplicable that Ministers and civil servants should have been allowed to get away with ignoring the priorities set out in a White Paper, particularly when all political parties have agreed to them. But that is what has happened to 'Custody, Care and Justice', written in 1991 after Lord Woolf's marvellous report into the 1990 riots in Manchester and elsewhere.

In his foreword to that Paper, the then Home Secretary, Kenneth Baker, said that it laid down a way forward that would take the Prison Service into the twenty-first century. What has happened to its 12 priorities? Precisely nothing, except to tighten security, which happened more as a result of the escapes from Whitemoor and Parkhurst, and to end slopping out, which was a separate initiative as well. It is salutary to remind ourselves of what was laid down and agreed ten years ago:

1 To improve necessary security measures.
2 To improve co-operation with other services and institutions, by working closely together with the Probation Service and by membership of a national forum and area committees.
3 To increase delegation of responsibility and accountability to all levels: with clear leadership and an annual statement of objectives.
4 To improve the quality of jobs for staff.
5 To recognize the status and particular requirements of unconvicted prisoners.
6 To provide active and relevant programmes for all prisoners, including unconvicted prisoners.

7 To provide a code of standards for conditions and activities in prisons, which will be used to set improvement targets in the annual contracts made between prison governors and area managers.

8 To improve relationships with prisoners, including a statement of facilities for each prisoner, sentence plans, consultations, reasons for decisions and access to an independent appeal body for grievances and disciplinary decisions.

9 To provide access to sanitation at all times for all prisoners.

10 To end overcrowding.

11 To divide the larger wings in prisons into smaller, more manageable units wherever possible.

12 To develop community prisons which will involve the gradual realignment of the prison estate into geographically coherent groups serving most prisoners within that area.

The list, including what should be done with and for both sentenced and unsentenced prisoners, remains unactioned, which undoubtedly contributes to the re-offending rates.

In his report, Lord Woolf also drew attention to the importance of keeping prisoners as near home as possible, so that both their families, and the community to which they will return, can be involved in their preparation for release. He gave figures to suggest that this had an impact on re-offending.

And what has happened about that? Again, precisely nothing. The Prison Service still persists with its archaic system of management, which makes one line manager responsible for all prisons in a geographic area, but mainly for budgets and compliance with targets and performance indicators. Only high-risk prisoners, women and children under the age of 18 have a separate policy branch that considers their treatment and conditions. But only in the case of high-security prisons, where most embarrassment to Ministers is presumed, does the person concerned have any control over the budgets of those prisons – the others have to 'horse-trade' for funds with geographic managers.

This of course leads to tremendous inconsistencies in the way that prisoners are treated. Some area managers give more priority to unsentenced than sentenced prisoners, and allocate funds accordingly. Some are attentive to the needs of young offenders, and others are not. Some take resettlement seriously, some do not. This is nothing other than a dangerous nonsense, working totally against the intention of the aim, putting financial niceties before the protection of the public. Responsible Ministers should see this, and challenge it. Of course budgets are important, but are they really more important than rectifying such obvious failure?

Again the solution has been created. This government has created a number of coterminous Criminal Justice System boundaries, within which courts, police, probation, social services, local government, education and health, as well as prisons, work to an Area Strategy Board, which can take account of local conditions. Lord Woolf talked about community clusters of prisons; in other words, sufficient prison places in each area, to house all prisoners of whatever type within the boundaries, with the possible exception of high-risk prisoners.

Of course such an introduction would require existing prisons to be re-roled, but that happens now with the recent announcement that a ninth adult male prison in five years is being converted to take women. But that such a move would prove to be a 'spend to save' measure goes without saying. At present 6,000 prisoners are held more than 150 miles from their homes, and a further 11,000 more than 100. Quite apart from affecting their resettlement, the Prison Service has to pay out millions of pounds each year in assisted family visits.

If I were able to do so, I would order the Prison Service to plan a re-roling programme now, to bring about such community clusters as soon as possible. I would appoint senior managers in each area, responsible for supporting governors of prisons with the local facilities that they need, to provide full, purposeful and active days for every prisoner, designed to challenge their offending or anti-social behaviour, or rectify those deficiencies that may be preventing them from living either useful or law-abiding lives.

At the same time, I would mirror the success of having a director of high security prisons, by appointing directors of each other type of prison, with their own budgets, responsible for ensuring consistency of treatment and conditions wherever prisoners for whom they are responsible are held. They would be accountable to the Director General, and ultimately the Home Secretary, Parliament and the public, for the re-offending rate in their prisons, being able to hold area managers to account for not providing satisfactory services.

What this would do would be to restore the old-fashioned principles of responsibility and accountability within a public service. Indeed, there can be no better example of how officials can be held to account for such an obvious failure rate as the current re-offending figures. Not only can individual prisons be identified, but individuals within prisons. Furthermore, such a structure would require directors to get out and lead, satisfying themselves that standards are being maintained, rather than do it by remote control through bureaucracy. What is more, sensible targets and performance indicators can be related to the real aim of protecting the public, rather than the bogus one of preventing Ministers from being embarrassed.

Had such a system been put in place by the first Prison Commissioner, I have no doubt that it would still be in use today. Throughout the twentieth century, the Prison Service was submitted to, or commissioned, a bewildering number of studies and reports, usually focusing on a disaster. Many recommendations were made, but, as is usual with such things, they did not tackle the whole problem.

As we start the twenty-first century, surely it is time to draw a line in the sand and say 'No more.' The action that I recommend is not just theory – everything that I have suggested is happening somewhere now, which highlights the unwillingness, or inability, of Prison Service management to turn good practice into common practice. I predict that, unless drastic action is taken, the present situation will continue to fail the public, and too many young offenders will see the shades of the prison house close on too many nights in their adult lives.

7 | **Prisoners and their Beliefs**

Jane Clay

'WHAT RELIGION ARE YOU?' is one of the questions that prisoners are asked when they are received into a new prison. The answers can be as varied as there are religions, but in my prison (a women's prison in West Yorkshire), most people say Church of England, Roman Catholic, Muslim or, increasingly among our younger prisoners, 'Nil.'

One of our chaplaincy team visits them very soon after they come to us and one of the things we have to do is to check whether or not their religion has been recorded correctly – often the confusion and distress they feel when they first come to prison means that they say anything that comes into their head, or even perhaps what they may have heard the person in front of them say. Those who have answered 'Nil' often admit to a clear belief in God but an unwillingness to own allegiance to a religion or church. Others are very sure that one of their family, often their grandmother, 'Nana', is a Christian and so they would like to be counted as that while they are in prison, perhaps as an insurance policy; more probably because they know that Nana is praying for them and they want to be part of that.

Prayer is very important to many of our prisoners. They are powerless and are devastated by their inability to care for their families. Most of them are mums. Some of our 16- and 17-year-olds have two or three children. (Of course they are children themselves – we look after girls as young as 15.) They love their babies and feel that if they can do nothing else they can pray for them. I have said this to some Christian groups and have been challenged, 'If these women really cared about their families they would not have broken the law in the first place.' If only it was that simple. They are offenders, and their offences have led to heartbreak and confusion for their children, but they still love them dearly, and one of the few things that they can do is pray for them. They pray in the quietness of their own room. They pray in corporate worship (well over half the prisoners come to chapel services and woe betide the chaplain if she forgets to leave a time of silence in the prayer time for individuals to remember those they love). They may not know how to pray, but they know that naming those they love in the sacred space that is the chapel is naming them before God and so is prayer.

They long to do something to express this prayerful concern and so we light many candles. Candles for joy, but more often for sorrow; candles for birth but more often for death. Always the candles are for love and take on a deeply spiritual conviction when lit in the chapel with prayer and placed on the altar to burn for several hours. Usually the prayer is put into words, sometimes by the prisoner, sometimes by the chaplain. I was praying with Nichola, who had lit a candle for Heather, who had died when injecting heroin into her groin. Nichola was crying too much to say anything herself and so I tried to express in a prayer something of what she might be feeling. During a pause, when I was struggling to find the next words, she said, 'That'll do Jane.' It was the best way of saying 'Amen' I have heard for a long time.

Many have a deep-rooted conviction that God will hear their prayer for other people. For many, there is an equally deep-rooted conviction that he will not consider their prayer for themselves. This is strongly related to their attitude to forgiveness. I think my colleagues in male prisons might have different stories to tell about this, as about many other things in this chapter, but women are often racked with remorse. They can just about understand that some victims may offer forgiveness (though forgiveness is not something any of us can ever require of another human), but the prisoners cannot forgive themselves for what they have done. This is not necessarily through empathy with their victim; they often lack that, which is why victim awareness work is so important. What they are completely aware of is the terrible effect their crime and imprisonment has on their families. One of the important roles a chaplain plays is to talk about the forgiveness of God which is freely offered to those who are sorry. An understanding of God's love and forgiveness may lead them to be able to forgive themselves and then to forgive others who have hurt them, and so contribute to a healing which may lead to a crime-free life on release.

I am constantly moved by the depth of prisoners' prayer for each other. One way of surviving in prison is to become selfish and uncaring of those around you, but many women choose to reach out to those who need love and care, and develop a deep generosity. They may only earn a few pounds each week, but will give each other cigarettes. We make endless cups of tea and coffee for people who come in for a chat. The prison does not supply that: we rely on the generosity of local Christians (God bless the Mothers' Union), but often a prisoner will bring some of her own hard-earned supplies. They pray out loud for each other, but in a way which does not break confidentiality. They often cry for each other. When a woman who has been part of our chapel family is leaving we always send her out with prayer. She comes to the front of chapel after our Holy Communion service and one or two (or sometimes a whole crowd) gather round her and lay hands on her and we send her out with God's blessing. Recently, we have been joined by some Jamaican women who have taught us that everyone in the group should stretch out their hands towards the one who is leaving. So that's what we do, without any self-consciousness and with as complete an understanding of 'laying on of hands' of any Christian group of which I've been a part. Touching and intimacy are very important to us. Many women in prison have been abused, and touch can feel very dangerous to them. In chapel we are restrained and careful about hugging, but rarely does someone shrug off a gentle touch on the arm. It seems important to reach out literally to someone who has just told you some intimate part of their life story, somehow to acknowledge the privilege that has been. All the people who are part of the chaplaincy team here at New Hall feel that we receive so much more from the women than we give.

Recently a whole group of the younger women started to come to Holy Communion. On Sunday, lots of women come to chapel (well over half the prison, not uncommon in a women's jail), but Monday night Holy Communion is a smaller group of more committed people. These new, younger women were being a bit disruptive – nothing serious, simply giggling and being silly. The older women value the peaceful, safe atmosphere in chapel and I held a separate meeting with them and offered to have a separate service with the younger ones. They were adamant: the young women must stay and we must change to accommodate them. I know that most churches would welcome any of our women who might want to join them, but I wonder if they would be as willing to change and accommodate those women as our own prisoners are.

I have pondered long on why so many come to chapel on Sunday morning. It's certainly not because they have all become committed church-going Christians, but it does have something to do with discovering spirituality. For many of them it is the first time they have stopped and thought about their lives. 'On the out' they have hectic, often chaotic lives which are all too often consumed by their drug or alcohol addiction. In prison they become clean from drugs; the responsibility of their families is taken from them; they don't have to 'graft' for their next fix and in this space they discover they are spiritual beings. They come to chapel to see if the chaplains can make sense of this, perhaps even give them a vocabulary to express what they are feeling. Most churches know that strangers who drop in for a service are often at crisis point. All women in prison are at crisis point; they come to chapel to see if the Church or even God has anything to say to them in their dilemma. The chapel is a place of beauty and stillness and offers peace.

I visited some of the women on our Detox Unit who had just arrived and were withdrawing from heroin and cocaine. I invited them to chapel. Other women in the room made a better job of inviting them than I did. 'Yes,' one said, 'come to chapel, you'll forget your rattle [withdrawal symptoms] for a little while.'

There is something very strong about the power of a caring community and a sharing of vulnerability. My mother died from cancer. While she was ill I asked the women to pray for us. Their fervency touched me, but not as much as their care did when I returned to work after her death. I could not walk a few yards in the prison before someone came up and said how sorry they were and gave me a hug. They understood, because loss and bereavement are often major parts of their lives. Their prayer is so natural. If someone does not wish to receive the bread and wine at Communion she will receive a prayer of blessing. I was praying with someone one day and at the end she looked me straight in the eye and said, 'The same to you, Jane.' I felt very prayed for! Often when a woman reaches desperation point she asks to come to chapel. It is because of the atmosphere of prayerfulness in the building, the sense of community and the practical way they show care to each other. I do not meet so many people in the church outside prison who really need the Christian family in the way some prisoners do.

Each Sunday we pray for the staff of the prison. Only once did someone hiss at this, and the others soon let her know that her reaction to praying for staff was completely unacceptable. On many occasions prisoners will ask for prayer for a particular officer on the wing who they know is experiencing a difficult time. One of our officers died recently. Some prisoners donated as much as 20 per cent of their meagre weekly earnings to a charity his wife had chosen.

For some, prayer is regarded as having magical properties. 'I go to court this week, Jane, pray that I'll get off.' My response? 'No chance, but I'll pray that you are treated with justice and compassion.' My Roman Catholic colleague is plagued with requests for rosary beads (called rosemary beads by everyone). There is a strong superstition around the possession of the beads which he works hard to combat. Often the women's approach is simple and superstitious, but for many of them it's a tentative moving towards God, which it is our responsibility as chaplains to nurture.

Occasionally someone comes to chapel who seems to understand only too well the power of prayer. I remember one woman who was convicted of a particularly nasty violent crime. She came to chapel with a strong Christian faith and a total conviction that God would open the prison gates for her in much the same miraculous way that he had when St Paul was in prison. Part of our job in the chaplaincy was to enable her to find a real freedom by facing up to her crime and truly repenting.

Every Sunday in our worship we say together a prayer in which we acknowledge what we have done to hurt other people, hurt ourselves and so hurt God. That prayer always includes the congregation, the person leading the services and even the officers at the back (though I'm not sure they always appreciate it). One Monday morning a woman asked to see me. She had been in the service and she said something strange had happened to her. She had suddenly realized the true impact of her offence on her family and had become overwhelmed with sorrow. She continued, 'Then I felt a real sense of everything being OK and a sort of warm feeling right over my body and I knew that God loved me.' It was my joy to tell her that she had experienced something that I never had, the physical presence of God through his Holy Spirit. I wish I could tell you what happened to her but she left the next day. The good thing is that we have never seen her again!

In our Christian chapel we always use Christian names. The women are sometimes called by their surnames and they always carry a number, but that is never referred to in chapel. One Maundy Thursday service several years ago was attended by a governor who is a Christian. We all went round and said our first names and he simply said, 'Mike.' A sense of oneness was created and no one ever took advantage of that gift he gave them that night. Prisoners, however can be very good at taking advantage. They sometimes take advantage of each other and can be very cruel to each other. On Ash Wednesday I offered each woman a tissue before she left chapel to wipe the ash from her forehead. I feared that they would face ridicule on the wing. None chose to take one, but all went back proudly wearing the Christian badge.

Tissues play a big part in our ritual. Chapel is a safe place and women often cry there. So do the chaplains. Prayer can unlock tears and when women weep there is always someone who will take the initiative, even in the middle of a service, bring her the tissues and comfort her. It has become just as important a part of our rite as is sharing the Peace in other places.

In prison it is very easy to become inward-looking. We have a team of volunteers from local churches who are part of the chaplaincy team and remind us that God's Church extends far beyond our prison fence. Our volunteers are marvellous. Some come in for a day a week and share in the enormous pastoral workload that there is. Women in prison bring with them all their concerns and hopes and fears, and they frequently want to talk. Sometimes they need professional intervention from our colleagues in the Probation or Psychology Departments, but often they just need a break, a cup of coffee (nice coffee and proper milk in the chapel), and someone to listen and care. Volunteers try to support them when things are rough with their family. They are there (along with the many other caring staff in the prison) when the women discover that they will not be allowed to care for their children when they are released. They share with them when they receive bad news from home, especially if it is news of a death. The volunteers listen when they talk about the abuse they have suffered. They try not to judge when they talk about the grim things they have done. They pray with them when they come to chapel to light a candle. They spend hours with them if they lose their equilibrium and end up on the segregation unit. The chaplaincy could not do this without the volunteer members of our team, and the prisoners often appreciate talking to someone who is not a paid member of staff carrying keys.

Other volunteers help lead groups or conduct worship. It is refreshing to have new ideas, different styles, other influences. A third group of volunteers come to join in worship and to let us know that we are part of Christ's worldwide Church. I would like to pay tribute to the Mothers' Union who offer us enormous support in chapel. We have an MU branch which two outside members lead. We run a parenting group which MU members support. The diocese gives us great support in this. It is led by the diocesan Family Life and Marriage Education (FLAME) officers. One of them is a man. I cannot exaggerate his importance or the importance of the other male members of the chaplaincy team. The women at New Hall need to meet safe men. The FLAME officer spends a great deal of time in the meetings modelling fathering. Many of our women have never been parented adequately themselves and so have no real insight into how to parent their own children. Indeed, they may have had horrendously negative experiences at the hands of their parents. Because of this I used to worry about talking about God as 'Father'. One day I was talking to one of our very committed Christian prisoners about my fears. I thought it would resonate with her because I knew she had received terrible treatment at the hand of her father. However, she was absolutely clear that she could easily understand the goodness of God's Fatherhood and that her understanding of this in some way helped to compensate for the terrible experiences she had.

Last June one of our long-term women came rushing into chapel clutching a letter. It was from a little girl who lives in Vukovar. Every year we join in 'Operation Christmas Child'. We pack shoe boxes full of gifts to send to children who would not otherwise receive a Christmas present. In the past our gifts have gone to the former Yugoslavia and last year they went to Afghanistan. Michelle had written a Christmas card for one of the boxes and included her name and address. Maria had written back to say 'Thank you'. It was a 'Thank you' to all of us, and of course we all cried! Nearly everyone in the prison takes part. Some knit or make beautiful hats, scarves, gloves or toys; some give sweets, toiletries, crayons and paper; the young offenders group make stunning Christmas cards; the workroom covers the shoe boxes in Christmas paper given by members of staff, who also bring in toys. By the time we sent our gifts to the local depot last year there must have been enough to fill nearly 200 shoe boxes. This is yet another example of the women's generosity and it also helps us to remember that although many of us are shut away we are still part of a much wider community, and the women here want to give what they can to others who are suffering too.

We sing a lot in chapel. We have a choir. There are no auditions: everyone who is willing is welcome. This sometimes causes problems. If the choir is sounding really good, as it often does, and then we are sometimes then joined by a 'groaner', some of the choir members feel that the music is spoilt. It is important to explain the inclusiveness of the choir in terms of the inclusiveness of God's kingdom. I used to worry that we had such a limited repertoire of hymns. We seem to sing the same ones over and over again, and the same half-dozen are always chosen if we have a request slot. Then I was walking round the prison one day and I heard one of the women singing one of our all-time favourites:

> Do not be afraid for I have redeemed you.
> I have called you by your name.
> You are mine.
> You are mine, O my child,
> I am your Father,
> And I love you with a perfect love.

I realized that they would probably forget most of what they heard in chapel, but they will not forget the words of the songs we sing so often that they become part of their being.

Some will never come to chapel. They tell me that they did not bother with God before prison so they will not take advantage of him now just because they want something. They treat God with enormous respect. They treat God's house with respect. People rarely swear in chapel. If they forget themselves, other women soon correct them. Older women care for the younger ones; they do not bully but they do exact a discipline in chapel to which the younger ones respond.

If prayer is real to the women, so is the reality of the story of Jesus. His story is so much more theirs than mine. Consider one who was 'grassed up' by a mate who was a paid police informer. He was then arrested during a police raid in the middle of the night and subjected to intimidating interrogation. He was brought before the court and remanded in custody. His friends abandoned him. He was brought before the court again and at some point subjected to police brutality. In the final trial, the judge who condemned him was weak and corrupt, intimidated by the prosecution and finally persuaded to pass the death sentence. In the light of Jesus's experience it's easy to see why prisoners relate to him so readily. They come to the Bible without any preconceptions; indeed they barely know the story of Jesus's life. On one Good Friday I told a group of women the story of Jesus's betrayal and death and finished the service by talking about his dead body being held by his mother. Then I said, 'But this is not the end, you'll have to come back on Sunday to hear what happened next.' As they left chapel I could hear women saying, 'I'm going to come back to find out!' Many of them do not have the first inkling about the resurrection of Jesus. Imagine my privilege of being the first person to say to them, 'He is not dead. He is risen.'

We had a Bible study group one evening when we looked at the story of the young Jesus being taken to Jerusalem by his parents for the feast. The group was predominantly people under 18. Bible study in the prison is so stimulating. The women are not afraid to say exactly what they think, because unlike a lot of other Christian groups they are not afraid of giving the wrong answers or of looking foolish. They don't know that there are any right answers! Their openness in a group is a joy. Having read the story I simply said, 'Well?' When preparing Bible studies in the prison I don't have to cudgel my brains to create stimulating open-ended questions to persuade reluctant participants to say something; the responses come tumbling out. The story relates that Mary and Joseph lost Jesus for three days. At least two women in that group had had their children taken into care because the authorities deemed that they neglected them. Their response was poignant. 'Mary and Joseph – rubbish parents!' Exactly what had been said of them in the past. Then we came to the part of the story which recorded Jesus's reply to Mary's challenge about his disappearance. 'Why were you searching for me? Did you not know that I must be in my Father's house?' This was too much for Jamie, who exclaimed, 'Blimey (or a similar word), cheeky bugger wasn't he?' Of course he was, but have you ever heard that expressed so clearly in church? Absolute honesty may not be the hallmark of much of the rest of their lives, but in discussion they specialize in being completely straightforward.

Recently one of the chaplains led a beautiful and powerful meditation which engaged our imaginations. After we had finished, people began to talk about what a rich and moving experience it had been, but after a while one young woman who has mental health problems said, 'I couldn't do it. It took too much concentration and I can't do that.' She said it without judgement or rancour, with no sense of inferiority, and she took the pressure off the rest of us who were feeling rather left out of this wonderful experience the others had had. I wish I could have been as honest in some of the groups of which I have been a part.

On another occasion, as part of baptism preparation we were discussing what baptism was for, and came to the conclusion that it had something to do with our response to the way God deals with sin in our lives. We looked at the story of Jesus and had a deeply theological and passionate discussion about whether or not Jesus had sinned. They did not know the Church's teaching and simply talked about the Jesus they knew. The discussion was inconclusive. Some were positive that he had sinned because they had such a grasp of his humanity, they felt that he was so much like them. Not long ago in a service I was telling them the story of Lazarus. Almost every Sunday the sermon is simply a retelling of one of the gospel stories. I told them all about a Jesus who understood human grief, about Mary and Martha who felt let down by a Jesus who healed all sorts of strangers but did not make the effort to arrive in time to heal his friend, and then I described the scene by the tomb. When I said that Lazarus came out of the tomb alive one of the women who had been completely engaged in the story could not help herself. She snorted out loud in derision. People do not come back from the dead. I treasure that honest response. The women I help care for totally understand the crucifixion; it's Easter Day they find hard to swallow.

Stories have the power to change lives. And the story of Jesus is the most powerful of all. The challenge is to show that resurrection can be as real for our prisoners as the pain and the suffering and the loss and the death are, so that Jesus's story can be even more compellingly theirs.

8 | Prisons: A Developing Chaplaincy

William Noblett

Introduction

The context and understanding of chaplaincy is changing. A developing chaplaincy, reflecting prisoner needs from all faith traditions, and none, is seeking to work in a collaborative, inclusive way. It seeks to bring together chaplains of all faith traditions to enable them to serve the needs of prisoners, staff and faith communities, inside and outside the prison. It is a time of re-definition and change as we seek to develop an understanding of ministry in prison, not just from a Christian perspective, but from that of the practitioners of different faith traditions. Prison ministry is on the frontier of inter-faith relationships, with considerable potential to offer an understanding of ministry in a multi-faith, multi-ethnic and secular organization, to faith communities beyond 'the walls'.

A developing chaplaincy will have to reflect on its understanding of how people of different faiths can live and work together in a closed environment, a 'total institution' (Goffman), while respecting the integrity of each tradition, and without seeking to impose patterns of ministry drawn from the majority tradition, and unthinkingly applied to those whose faith and world-view presents something different. It will require a developing understanding of both theoria and praxis. It will involve a paradigm shift. David Bosch wrote in his monumental work, *Transforming Mission*, that 'a paradigm shift always means both continuity and change, both faithfulness to the past and boldness to engage the future, both constancy and contingency, both tradition and transformation . . .' that it will be 'both evolutionary and revolutionary'. Such a transition, 'from one paradigm to another', he says, 'is not abrupt', and the agenda is always one of 'reform, not replacement', with 'creative tension between the new and the old'. The chaplaincy has enormous potential to hold 'tradition and transformation' in creative tension, and to be at the heart of a developing praxis of ministry in prison. At its core is the need to support individuals in their spiritual quest, reflected in the Chaplaincy Statement of Purpose:

> HM Prison Service Chaplaincy is committed to serving the needs of prisoners, staff and faith communities by engaging all human experience through religious faith and practice. We will work collaboratively, respecting the integrity of each tradition and discipline.

We believe that faith directs and inspires life, and are committed to providing sacred spaces and dedicated teams to nurture the human spirit so that it may flourish and grow. By celebrating the goodness of life and exploring the human condition we aim to cultivate in each individual a responsibility for contributing to the common good.

Historical context

The historical context and understanding of Christian ministry in prisons, however, cannot be ignored, and I begin with a brief introduction to that history.

In the Licence given by each Anglican bishop to those priests who minister within his diocese, are the words, 'Receive the cure of souls, which is both mine and yours.' For me, these are powerful words, bestowing on both parties a responsibility for shared ministry in the prison context. The bishop represents the wider Church of which we are but one part. Christians who minister in prison have a responsibility to the Church. The Church's presence in English and Welsh prisons has been officially recognized since 1773, when an Act of Parliament authorized Justices of the Peace to appoint salaried chaplains to their local prisons. The salary was not to exceed £50 per annum, and was to come from the county rates.

It may be a surprise to some, but up until this time, most jails were privately run, including one or two under the control of bishops. The profit motive meant that prisoners were charged fees for the services provided for them while in prison. In the Fleet Prison, made famous by

Charles Dickens, charges were on a sliding scale, with an Archbishop expected to pay an entrance fee of £10. At that time, few were willing to pay for the services of a clergyman, and formal acts of worship took place infrequently. With the introduction of salaried chaplains, the situation slowly changed. Interestingly, the opening of the Wolds Prison in April 1992 brought to an end a period of over 100 years in which all prisons in the United Kingdom had been directly managed by central government. Private sector management within the penal system had returned.

In the nineteenth century, clergy were at first appointed on a part-time basis and they had a purely pastoral role. In recent times the former Archbishop of Canterbury, Robert Runcie, reiterated this role:

> In talking to prison chaplains I have emphasized their pastoral role. This is in line with the commission given to bishops, priests and deacons of the Church of England at their ordination, when the pastoral emphasis is overwhelming; they are to provide for the flock and to minister to the sheep who have gone astray.

The first chaplains attended to the sick and those about to be executed, but some found their task depressing and unrewarding. Complaints arose that such men could not do much in a prison which echoed with profaneness and blasphemy. The same might be thought true today. But ministry is partly about faithfulness, perseverance, the continuous and renewed call to be where God's people are, in whatever circumstances.

The office and role of chaplain was given much greater significance following the powerful influence and advocacy of John Howard, whose famous book *The State of the Prisons in England and Wales* appeared in 1777. John Howard had visited prisons in Holland where services were regularly held in a prison chapel. Howard urged that similar arrangements should be made in English prisons, and he made a plea to jailers not to hinder prisoners from attending 'divine worship'. Robert Peel's Gaol Act of 1823 gave more careful definition of the responsibilities of the chaplain, and made it possible for the stipend to be as much as £250 per annum.

Between 1816 and 1877, central government had responsibility only for convict prisoners, and when the first of these prisons, Millbank, opened in 1816, the church's mission with prisoners was given much greater stimulus. In Millbank, which was designed to hold 1,000 prisoners, the atmosphere was very different from that which had prevailed in the much smaller county jails. The experiment was firmly built on the conviction that evangelism was the answer to crime. The chapel stood at the very heart of the penitentiary, and this was to provide chaplains with a unique opportunity. The authorities directed that every prisoner must attend religious services and must behave reverently in chapel. Going one step further, they even made the chaplain the governor of the establishment. He was able to order the programme to suit his avowed aim, and all the rules were geared to achieve the object of religious exercises, by which the convicts would be reformed. Each warder (now called prison officers) carried a Bible, and was expected to quote scripture at appropriate moments.

The experiment was not considered a success, however, and it proved that even the coercion of the penitentiary cannot bring about change without a heart which is open to the love of God.

Other prisons were soon to follow at Parkhurst, Portland and Dartmoor. In 1842, Pentonville Prison was opened. Known as the Model Prison, it was the first of 54 prison buildings constructed to a similar design during the next six years, and of which most are still in use today. As we have seen so often, the model was taken from the American experience, and transported to England. Essentially a system of solitary confinement for all prisoners, it relied on discipline carried to extreme lengths. It came from Pennsylvania, where faith in the value of solitude as a means of reforming criminals was almost fanatical. Prisoners were placed in cells, and could be shut off from human companionship for many years – a situation still experienced by prisoners in oppressive regimes in some countries, even today. The prisoners stayed in their cells for divine worship, many desperately trying to catch sound of a human voice, with the preacher standing in the corridor. In American 'super-max' prisons, Sunday worship is conducted by television linkage to each cell.

At the time, the deprivation of human fellowship was designed to encourage communion with God. Reminiscent of monks in their cells, it has been suggested that the concept of prison as we know it came from a monograph written by a seventeenth-century Benedictine monk, in which he recommends that wrongdoers be reformed by sampling a spell of monastic life. In the 'model prison' the chaplain's role was a major one. To men desperate for companionship, he was to dispense the consolation of the Gospel.

The task proved to be impossible. Even with an assistant, it was not easy to get around all the cells, and eventually a compromise was agreed. The prisoners would be taken to chapel on Sundays for worship, but in order to maintain their isolation, they were made to wear hoods over their heads, and to sit in individual boxes during the service, so they could see the preacher, but not each other.

Eventually, this system of solitary confinement, which had partly come about as a protest against the indiscriminate herding of all kinds of prisoners in enforced cohabitation, gave way to one of classification and training, much as we know it today.

The chaplain's role, however, continued to be enshrined in the various Prison Acts, up to and including that of 1952, the most recent. In a sense, the pastoral role of which Lord Runcie spoke has become part of the requirement placed on chaplains through what are called 'Statutory Duties', contained both within the Act and in various Prison Rules. Effectively, they are what most chaplains would see as being important pastorally as they involve seeing prisoners as they come into the prison (Receptions), and daily if they are in the Segregation Unit, the Health Centre or the Vulnerable Prisoner Unit. Additionally, people are seen in their cells, at worship, their workplace, or in groups. No member of the chaplaincy team is limited by that which is defined as 'statutory', and these duties are but the springboard to involvement with the whole life of the prison, in different ways, and at different levels, with prisoners and staff, and their families.

Brian Dodsworth, a former chaplain, describes chaplains as 'standing at the cross-roads of human experience, able to meet with men and women, often in crisis'. Sense needs to be made of their waiting, their pain and, perhaps, their guilt. Prison represents an extreme human experience, and it is here that people sometimes encounter God, with joy and hope, and occasionally with a sense of sins forgiven.

The ministry to those in prison will always take various forms, but the purpose must be to proclaim something of the unconditional love of God. It is not about being in a position to moralize, to impose a particular viewpoint: it is about encouraging a process of growth and self-discovery, which may take much time. For many chaplains, they can only 'plant the seed' and hope and pray that it will be nurtured.

We have to hold to the conviction that, however desolating an experience it may be, prison can be a stimulus to provoke real choices, and transformation of lives. At the heart of each person who ministers in prison (with a theistic understanding), there is a faith rooted in the reality and purpose of God, in whom all things are possible.

Christian chaplains are called by God, and by the Church, to a shared ministry in a difficult place. Their task is the joyful proclamation of the love of God, and they are in prison to be used, to be accessible and available to give simple, and sometimes costly, care. Brian Dodsworth writes, 'Unless imprisonment can become part of a journey toward a goal rather than a desert of purposeless waiting, the chaplain's help is of limited value. Endless patience is required to stay present with people who cannot yet choose a road – for, in the end, it can never be chosen for them' (Dodsworth 1989).

A changing environment

In March 2002, the prison population reached a record 70,000. Ten years ago it was 42,000, with 31,000 registered in a Christian denomination. Now, with a population of 70,000, those registered as Christian make up 40,000. We currently employ some 140 full-time Christian chaplains, a further 19 full-time assistant chaplains (Christian), 119 part-time Christian chaplains and some 350 on a sessional basis (i.e. who regularly attend for between two and ten hours). Ten years ago, just over 2,000 prisoners were registered as Muslim. Now that number has reached 5,071. We have started to employ some full-time imams, and will soon have six. There are 107 imams employed on a sessional basis. Ten years ago there were 1,000 prisoners registered in other world faiths. Now that figure is 1,300, and we have ministers from all recognized faith traditions. The largest area of 'growth' has been among those registered as 'Nil Religion'. Ten years ago the figure was 7,500, now it is over 22,000. Against this background, many people feel the chaplaincy has got to develop a fairer and more inclusive way of working. The historic allocation of resources to chaplaincy teams has led to some imbalances, and while the reasons for these are understandable in the context of the time, they need to be reviewed in the light of changing circumstances. Within a publicly funded organization, the chaplaincy will want to ensure that the recent definition of 'institutional religionism', produced by the University of Derby, is acknowledged and action taken to deal with any shortcomings there may be. The report, commissioned by the government, examined forms of religious discrimination. It suggests that there exists a range of behaviour and attitudes linked to the unfair treatment of people on the basis of religion or race. It speaks of 'institutional religionism', saying it

> . . . can be understood . . . as the product of a combination of several factors into a mutually reinforcing environment and ethos. 'Institutional religionism' thus occurs in a context in which 'religious prejudice', 'direct' and 'indirect' religious discrimination combine in the collective failure of an organisation to provide an adequate and professional environment and service. Negligence and indifference often contribute to this failure. (Weller, Feldman and Purdham 2001)

The chaplaincy will also want to take account of the Human Rights Act, the Race Relations Amendment Act, and the European Union directive on religious discrimination, to be implemented by the end of 2003. All of these factors will influence change and the direction of chaplaincy. It will also want to develop its understanding of the theology of religions, inter-faith dialogue, racial justice and the sharing of resources, because it is right that we should do so. David Haslam, a Methodist minister and part-time chaplain, has written, 'Christianity offers no easy way, and when Christians seek to avoid analysis, and engagement with the oppressed, they are avoiding the strategy and methodology of the Kingdom' (Haslam 1996).

The development of an inclusive approach, however, building on positive aspects of the past, could enhance the existing credibility of many chaplaincies. Far from this leading to marginalization, it could help place the chaplaincy at a more significant place in the prison community. The perception of a team of people of different faiths, of varied ethnicity, holding each other, and those with whom they work, in mutual respect and regard and working for the common good, can offer an insight into world faiths that is a model for good relationships in prison, and in wider faith communities. It also contributes to our recognition and celebration of diversity. While I was chaplain at

HMP Full Sutton, I led, with my imam colleague, a weekly session on an Introduction to Race Relations for prisoners. It provided a tiny glimpse of 'how things might be', a counter-cultural model, to staff and prisoners, some of whom may live in, or return to, areas with the sort of racial tensions manifested in the summer of 2001 – to Bradford, Burnley or Oldham. And in the reception area of Leeds Prison, where prisoners, many arriving in prison for the first time, are at a vulnerable point, a member of the chaplaincy team is available to provide a 'listening ear', in a way different from uniformed staff. Each prisoner is seen by a member of the chaplaincy up until 9 p.m., and the potential contribution to helping prisoners adapt to their situation is enormous. But this service, for the common good, could not be done without the active participation of the two part-time imams, the Mormon minister, and other members of the team. Such a way of working, I believe, is a reflection of our respective faiths being lived out in a place where positive role models are in short supply. At a time when the Home Secretary, David Blunkett, is calling for a 'conversation between faith and politics', we need to develop the conversation between faith and the penal system, using the opportunity to re-evaluate what it is that faith can offer to the penal system and the people living and working within it, but which, conversely, has something to offer to people of faith in the wider community.

A further illustration, from my recent experience of being Church of England chaplain at HMP Full Sutton, a high-security establishment near York, may help. At Full Sutton, we developed an inclusive, multi-faith team. It may be useful to start by saying what it was not. It was not 'inter-faith' in the sense that we had little theological dialogue at anything other than a personal level – we spent most of our time working on practicalities – on the issues necessary for a fair and equitable approach to ministry for all faiths within a publicly funded organization. It was not a move to syncretism, a diminishment of the uniqueness of Christ.

It was not a move to inter-faith worship – in which the lowest common denominator may sometimes become normative, and frustrate everyone. The nearest we ever got to inter-faith worship was on Good Friday when, in the chapel, we commemorated the crucifixion and death of Christ, while a few metres away our brothers in Islam said their Jumma/Friday prayers; and on the night of the Carol Service when we sang carols in the Chapel as the Muslims said Ramadan prayers in the multi-faith room. Afterwards we all enjoyed mutual sharing – of mince pies.

This is not to trivialize, but is to point to the need to respect the boundaries, to enable worship, the giving of worth to God, and each other – whatever the tradition – while at the same time offering the hospitality which is so much part of our Christianity, rooted in the hospitality of Abraham to the angels at Mamre, and in our understanding of the relationality implicit in our understanding of the Triune God. I have no desire to be a Muslim, a Sikh, or any other tradition, and I respect those of such traditions who may have no desire to be a Christian. I am what Archbishop George Carey has described as 'an approachable separatist – someone who is secure in their own faith, but values contact and conversation with other faith communities, and believes such contact will not result in any fundamental changes to his own beliefs, but may lead to a greater degree of understanding'. And in a very Trinitarian way, I believe that God calls us to realize ourselves in relationship – and in the confines of a prison, that can only be done with all faith traditions, and with none. In the words of David Bosch, I live with 'the abiding paradox of asserting both ultimate commitment to one's own religion, and genuine openness to another's' (Bosch 1991).

So why do we need to move to an inclusive chaplaincy, nationally and locally? The Prison Act of 1952 states that the chaplain, or any assistant chaplain, will be a clergyman of the Church of England – with prison ministers of other denominations being invited in as necessary. A reflection of our society at the time – with a prison population that had few people who registered as other than Church of England, Roman Catholic, Methodist or Jew.

Time has changed all of that, in society, as in prison – as earlier figures have shown. As we know, Christian ecumenism has developed in a very positive way – inside and outside the prison. Despite the structures of the Act, we do have full-time Roman Catholic chaplains and a few Free Church. In some ways, how we now see faiths other than Christianity in prison is analogous to the way Anglicans once viewed Roman Catholics and Methodist participation in this publicly funded chaplaincy. Christian ecumenical co-operation can, paradoxically, make multi-faith involvement more difficult for different faiths. In some subtle, unintentional and for the most part unrecognized ways, such a situation has developed in prison chaplaincy – and is reflected in the disparity of resource allocation I mentioned earlier. It is reflected, too, in the way we have seen ministers from different faiths as 'visiting ministers' – a term once applied to Roman Catholic and Methodist chaplains; a term which enforces a sense of 'exclusion', of not being part of the system, despite, for example, some prisons having a very high number of Muslim prisoners. It is shown in such things as the automatic issuing of keys to Christian chaplains, no matter that they are only in the prison for a few hours, while denying keys to those of different faiths spending more time in the prison – an attitide which is about much more than diminished mobility; in the assumption sometimes conveyed by a few chaplains that the budget is 'Christian', despite its public funding – with implications for how we enable other people with a legitimate ministry to their prisoners, and with a ministry which may be part of the *missio Dei*. It is continued in many other ways too numerous to mention, but summed up in some of the indications of institutional discrimination:

- the preferential treatment of majorities;
- limited, or no training for minorities;
- inattention to minority affairs;
- the withholding of information from specific groups and the use of majority standards for all behaviour.

All done unwittingly, perhaps, but since the Macpherson Report that, too, is unacceptable. The government and the Prison Service are aware of the implications that arise from this sort of situation. As the number of people in prison continues to rise, so too will the demands of ministry to a disparate group, and it will have to be addressed. And as the leading representatives of the Sikh, Buddhist and Muslim communities continue to campaign for the improvement of religious and pastoral care for their prisoners, their voices are being heard, and change is being demanded. The keen interest of the British Commission on Islamaphobia, pressure groups, minority faith communities, and some governors who see this as an issue of justice, add significantly to the debate.

The model for the future, however, has yet to be clearly worked out and is, as the title of this chapter implies, a 'developing' model. Martin Narey, Director General of the Prison Service, has said:

I think one of the things the Prison Service had been doing well for many years, is providing spiritual and pastoral care for Christians who are in our care. I think we have a much poorer story to tell about catering for the spiritual and other needs of those from non-Christian faiths . . . The new Chaplain General will have a precise brief to care for the welfare of all faiths and not just the Christian faiths. We need to give a better deal to minority faiths if we are to assure those in custody that they will get a fair deal.

Part of what I am required to do in my role is to address that new direction at national, as well as local, level. For the first time, a Chaplain General is tasked to specifically care for the provision necessary for all faiths – reflecting some words by Hooker and Lamb in *Love the Stranger: Ministry in Multi-Faith Areas*: 'Hopefully, there is now a deeper recognition in Britain that adherents of many religions now co-exist here and that they must be given the respect and freedom traditionally enjoyed by the established church. Indeed, we would claim that only if the Church of England actively promotes respect and freedom for others can its privileged position still be justified.' The reality is that many chaplaincies already function in ways that do enable and encourage different faith traditions – in positive and encouraging engagement, and in close working for the common good.

The core principles on which the ministry of the Team at Full Sutton is based, and which are suitable for wider application, are:

- the recognition and celebration of diversity;
- respect for the integrity of each tradition;
- the value of each member being affirmed;
- a giving and accepting of responsibility;
- empowerment, through the recognition of each chaplain's ministry;
- the principles and practice of RESPOND, RESPECT – Prison Service initiatives to combat racism and discrimination, and to promote positive Race Relations, and the inter-faith Network Guidelines, are integral to all that is done;
- decision-making, whenever possible, is that of the Team and done in a collegial way;
- the allocation and re-allocation of budget resources is 'transparent' and a Team responsibility;

- Team members believe chaplaincy must show an alternative way of working within the institution, and serve as a positive example to staff and prisoners;
- people, not power, lies at the heart of the chaplaincy;
- collaborative working is seen as the norm;
- accountability is mutual;
- communication is open and honest.

These principles, and the sense of direction we shared, came from a process of consultation – of dialogue, of listening.

I have already started a similar process of consultation at national and Area level, involving chaplains and ministers of all faith traditions full-time, part-time and sessional. I also want to hear from faith leaders beyond the walls. The direction has been set by Martin Narey and the Prison Service Management Board, reflecting elements of government policy. How we get there is down to us, collectively and collaboratively, as we seek to serve the needs of prisoners, staff and faith communities.

Collaborative ministry has undergirded my own approach to ministry since I joined the Prison Service – and it has some implications for my understanding of the place of the Prison Service chaplaincy in the missiology of the Church of England.

I want to introduce:

- a chaplaincy more 'rooted' in Prison Service Areas, and the local context of faith communities. Part of the way in which this will be done is through a process that enhances the role of Area Chaplains and furthers the principles of devolution and subsidiarity. Such a move will reshape Chaplaincy Headquarters, its function, and staffing;
- a closer link between chaplains and the wider Church, reflected in the way appointments are made;
- in the way we do our theology – for we have much to offer from within the walls, and much to learn;
- in the links with Diocesan Order and Law groups and other voluntary groups who make such a contribution to prison life – and could make more;
- in the way those links can be developed as prisoners are prepared for release, and subsequently supported by faith communities, where appropriate.

At a time when many speak of the secularization of institutions – seen as part of the postmodernist process – chaplaincy in the Prison Service can make a significant contribution to our understanding of what it means to be a human being, created somehow in the image of God, but living and working in the prison context. I believe that an inclusive chaplaincy, committed to serving prisoners, staff and faith communities, can be a presence of great significance, building on the firm base already established by chaplains. It is a pivotal time for us, and for those we serve. The Jesus Christ whom I seek to follow took the form of a servant in order to do the will of God, and I feel privileged to be called to serve at this time.

Conclusion

Without a challenge to the inequities which are part of the structures of power, and which have been revealed in the Macpherson, Derby and other Reports, injustices may prevail and structures remain inert. Haslam has reminded us that Jesus was crucified because of his 'challenge to those in power – spiritual power as much as temporal power – because they had ceased to try to make things right, to struggle for justice, even within the confines of the Roman occupation' (Haslam 1996). I believe that the chaplaincy can play its part in 'making things right', in bringing hope. But hope is not a strategy, and strategic planning is necessary to set the direction for the future. Such a strategy must reflect religious and racial justice, encounter and dialogue. Far from relativism, or syncretism, it places relationships and faithfulness at the heart of a developing understanding of ministry in prison. As such it reflects a gospel imperative.

As part of our response to diversity, in a society where there is a widely accepted commitment to freedom of religious conviction and practice, Christians need to be more aware of the needs of minorities, to hear their voice, and to respond appropriately. Minority religions have more limited influence in many areas of public life, particularly in well-established institutional contexts such as the Prison Service. We need to acknowledge 'institutional racism' and 'institutional religionism' before we begin to eradicate them. The Right Reverend Tom Butler, Bishop of Southwark, responding to the Macpherson Inquiry Report in a 1999 article entitled 'Time to see ourselves as others see us', highlights this need. Butler wrote, 'The point of institutional racism is that, whether or not the organisation is made up of good people without individual racism, the organisation works to the disadvantage of people from ethnic minorities.' Calling on the Church of England to recognize and acknowledge its racism, he says, '. . . the truth is that none of our institutions can bear too much scrutiny – they all suffer from institutional racism'. We 'need to see ourselves as other see us', before we can begin the process of change. The evangelist, Mike Riddell, has written, 'Wherever you find yourself in life, the answer to your questions always lies in pressing forward into the unknown, never in moving backwards.' For the chaplaincy to continue 'pressing forward' would be a fitting tribute to Bishop Bob.

References

Bosch, David J., *Transforming Mission: Paradigm Shifts in Theology of Mission.* Orbis Books, Maryknoll, NY, 1991.

Butler, Tom, 'Time to see ourselves as others see us', *Church Times*, 19 March 1999.

Carey, George, 'How far can we travel together? Facing the issues of interfaith dialogue', *World Faiths Encounter*, 16, 1997.

Dodsworth, Brian, *Ministry to Prisoners in London.* Dioceses of London and Southwark Penal Affairs Group, 1989.

Haslam, David, *Race for the Millennium: A Challenge for Church and Society*, Church House Publishing, London, 1996.

Narey, Martin, talk given at a Prison Service Race Relations Officer Conference.

Riddell, Mike, quoted in Steve Chalke, 'The journey', *Oasis News.*

Runcie, Robert, *Reform, Renewal and Rehabilitation.* Prison Reform Trust 1990.

Weller, Paul, Feldman, Alice, and Purdham, Kingsley, *Religious Discrimination in England and Wales.* Research Study 220. Home Office 2001.

9 | The Prisoner as Volunteer: A New Model of Self-help

Myra Fulford

THE CATHOLIC SOCIAL SERVICE for Prisoners, founded in 1898 by two Catholic lawyers as an expression of their Christian faith and commitment, was just one example of the great flowering of Victorian philanthropy in the nineteenth century; it was an era when private citizens were particularly busy establishing charities to meet any and every need and at a time when it would have been inconceivable that the state should provide health care, housing or services for poor children and families. The pattern of welfare provision during that era was one of philanthropy and paternalism.

In 1985, the Catholic Social Service for Prisoners changed its name and became the Bourne Trust. The charity had always provided services to all, irrespective of their creed, but in the increasingly secular times of the late twentieth century it was felt that to retain the word 'Catholic' in the name was misleading. In October 2001, the Bourne Trust merged with a smaller charity, Prisoners' Wives and Families Society (PWFS), which had been established in 1975 from a personal experience of imprisonment. The merged organization, Prison Advice and Care Trust (PACT), is committed to maintain both the Christian impulse of the Bourne Trust and the self-help ethos of PWFS in its work in that they both proclaim the value and potential of the individual.

Bob Hardy, Bishop of Lincoln and Bishop to Prisons, became known, among other reasons, for his excellent work in bringing voluntary organizations and faith groups working in prisons together and giving them a voice. He was one of the catalysts for the establishment in 1998 of CLINKS (which aims to promote the rehabilitation of offenders by improving the links between prisons and the voluntary and community-based sector in England and Wales), and in 2000 the creation of the post of Voluntary Sector Co-ordinator at Prison Service Headquarters, and the establishment of the Prison Service Voluntary and Community Sector Strategy Group. It might, at this juncture, be useful to review the role and *modus operandi* of the voluntary sector throughout the twentieth century; it might also be valuable to ascertain whether, at the beginning of the twenty-first century, there is a continuing role for the sector as the provider of services for prisoners and their families both during the custodial period and on resettlement into the community on release – and if so, what that distinctive role and contribution might be.

Broadly speaking, in the first half of the twentieth century, charitable organizations provided the lion's share of welfare provision. As early as 1870, the Education Act committed the state to universal provision of elementary education, but it was only after the Second World War that the Labour government of the day passed a raft of legislation which would create the welfare state and a system of cradle-to-grave benefits provided by the state. Beveridge, already regarded as father of the welfare state, was concerned that all these changes would impact on and change the role of the voluntary sector:

> . . . room, opportunity and encouragement must be kept for voluntary action in seeking new ways of social advance . . . There is a need for political intervention to find new ways of fruitful co-operation between public authorities and voluntary agencies. (Beveridge 1948)

Despite Beveridge's concerns, the long tradition of socialist opposition to voluntarism – a feeling that voluntary work was the perk and prerogative of the middle class and as such masked the need for paid work – prevailed in the immediate post-war period.

It was only in the 1960s, with the growth of feminism, black power and identity politics that the voluntary sector began to assert itself in a new way and was the key driver to putting green and environmental issues, through the work of Greenpeace and Friends of the Earth in the 1970s and 1980s, onto the political agenda. Charities set up at the turn of the century to provide services for disabled people found themselves in the 1970s and 1980s facing a tide of opposition from people with disabilities. People with disabilities no longer wanted to be defined by them.

By way of example, Kingston Association for Disabled People

became in 1986 Kingston Association *of* Disabled People and in 2001 became Kingston Centre for Independent Living. These name changes were not cosmetic: they announced a new and growing confidence in some key people with disabilities in Kingston upon Thames and resulted in effective and finally successful campaigning. Kingston upon Thames Social Services Department was the first local authority in England and Wales to make disability living allowance payments to people registered disabled in the borough: this enabled them to purchase their own care packages, to employ their own carers and to live independently. This innovative and empowering practice has spread, but it is interesting to note that this change, to treating people with physical disabilities as equal citizens, did not occur until the end of the twentieth century and that change only came about as a result of voluntary sector activity.

In 1975 the Royal Institute for the Blind (RNIB) had an Executive Council of 120, of whom only eight were blind (shortly before that only two on the Executive Council were blind). A subsequent review offered a further four places to blind people. The National Federation of the Blind campaigned and it was accepted that one third of the Executive Council should be registered blind. RNIB has now accepted the principle of user representation and is moving towards 50 per cent of the Council being users. These policy changes in the largest charity providing services for blind people are significant and will, over a period of time, change society's perception of blind people and, as importantly, change the style and nature of the services provided by the charity.

> . . . if you want to do something about blindness, you have to talk to blind people. In the past they would have just pushed ahead. Within RNIB and other organisations there is much more of an awareness that you cannot do this in the way it was done in the past. (Low)

And it was the voluntary sector in the form of Councils for Racial Equality which began calling local authorities to account in the 1970s for their recruitment practices with regard to minority communities, in their lack of ethnic monitoring of delivery of services to these communities and the absence of any written Equal Opportunities Policy to inform their practice.

One cannot be sanguine or complacent about what has or has not been achieved in the intervening 30 years, but merely make the point that the catalyst for action came from the voluntary sector and the minority communities themselves, and that awareness was raised and some small victories won.

The same political shift took place in the mental health voluntary sector, but not until some ten years later. The Manic Depression Fellowship (MDF) was set up in 1983 by parents and carers of people who had a diagnosis of manic depression (bi-polar affective disorder). The majority of trustees were carers, with only two token mental health service users chosen by carers and not elected by the membership. In 1992 there was a 'palace coup' and an election for membership of the Council of Management which returned a near 100 per cent user majority. This paradigm shift resulted in increased confidence in their own skills on the part of the membership, a recognition of the potential for individuals to learn and develop strategies for managing episodes of mental ill health, and a significant growth in the membership of the charity. In 1992 MDF gained funding from the Department of Health and the King's Fund to develop and research a Self-Management Training Programme to be delivered by trainers who had a diagnosis of manic depression and who had successfully self-managed their mental health over the previous five years.

The above are random powerful examples of the voluntary sector providing the opportunity for people to get together, to speak out, to take power and to demand that they are recognized first and foremost as citizens, as legitimate and equal stakeholders in society, as people who will only be disempowered if defined by their diagnosis, their physical disabilities, their learning difficulties, the colour of their skin or their gender.

We would argue that this political shift from less paternalistic provision to more enabled and empowered users of services and a re-definition of users of public services as customers has not yet occurred in prisons. Working with prisoners and their families is demanding work; the majority of society would prefer not to think about the complicated issues of imprisonment – they prefer the populist sound-bites of the daily press.

Up until 2000 no governing Prime Minister had ever visited a prison, and of the Members of Parliament who had a prison within their constituency, only one in four had visited (Levenson 1998). Most prisons, by their very nature, are inward-looking, inflexible establishments; prisoners in custody are removed from society, and anyone trying to visit a prison will find it almost as difficult to get in as it is to get out! When society and the community abdicate responsibility in this way for what happens in prisons, the system turns in on itself, becomes 'a world apart', and as such almost immune to political shifts in society. This will affect styles of working, attitudes to gender, race, sexuality and modes of communication.

It was in the 1970s that Councils of Racial Equality were calling local authorities to account for the inadequacy of their responses to minority communities. It was nearly 30 years later that RESPOND (Race Equality for Staff and Prisoners) was unveiled at the 1999 Prison Service Annual Conference by the then Director General, Richard Tilt; and Judy Clements was appointed as the Prison Service's first Race Equality Adviser. Clements, in an interview for the *Prison Service News* (*PSN*), commented:

> Like all parts of the Criminal Justice System we have a long way to go. I must confess that things are a lot worse than I had expected. I think that if we can . . . break down some of the barriers in how we treat each other, then I think the way we treat prisoners irrespective of their ethnicity will go a long way to reflecting the kind of Service that the Director General, Martin Narey, and his Management board wants. It is about treating people, not just prisoners, humanely.
>
> Most of it is pretty blatant. It's not even subtle. There is a sense of not even caring. If that is at peer group level then there is the issue of how prisoners are treated.
>
> It is particularly disturbing stuff. The things that are said to prisoners and then denied like 'Why do you need a phone card? There are no telephones in Africa' or 'Why don't you go back to Africa?' The obvious 'n' word is constantly used and I find it absolutely frightening. (Clements 2000)

It is not only black people that are treated with such disrespect. It is endemic.

In his opening speech at the Prison Service Conference 2002 the Director General, Martin Narey, said:

> Our increasingly overcrowded prisons are not humane, healthy environments where prisoners can take responsibility for their offending behaviour, gain skills and start the process of rehabilitation and become contributing citizens . . . no one, including me, thinks that locking more and more people up is a sensible way of spending public money. Many of the people we are locking up will not benefit in any way from their sentence. Many of them will lose jobs, accommodation and family support and will become more criminal . . . The harsh reality is that when we go to the Treasury with a bid for resources for thousands more additional prison places . . . the probability of . . . getting the investment to make prisons the decent and reformative places we know they can be, is bleak.

Anne Owers, Chief Inspector of Prisons, writes in the Preface to HM Inspectorate of Prisons Report on Unannounced Inspection of HMP Dartmoor, September 2001:

> We discovered a prison which was itself imprisoned in its own past – locked into unsuitable but historic buildings and, more importantly, into an outdated culture of over-control and disrespect for prisoners . . . Dartmoor is a lesson in how negative cultures can take hold, or re-establish themselves, if a prison does not have a positive vision . . . the overwhelming impression, during our inspection, was of a lack of respect. This was pervasive. Many officers (even those in management roles) made it clear to us, and in audible conversation with each other, that they had no respect for management, either within the prison or the Prison Service. Nor did they feel that management had respected them, or communicated with them. But the main victims of the lack of respect were the prisoners. They were described directly to us as the 'rubbish', 'these people' or 'coloureds'; or alternatively as people who were too dangerous to engage with.

Erwin James is serving a life sentence and now, in a resettlement prison, regularly contributes to the *Guardian*. In February 2002 he was asked to show a group of visiting psychology students around the prison.

> Looking through their eyes, I could see that what had been pre-sented was a seemingly pleasant environment . . . apparently free from the pressures of 'real life'. It was important that they under-stood . . . 'This is a resettlement prison', I said: 'It is in no way representative of the general prison system.'
>
> . . . I did not want to paint too bleak a picture of the system as a whole; I . . . had benefited greatly from my years in prison. Never-theless, my view was that that was mainly in spite of the system . . . The knowledge of what time inside can do to people – the knowledge that can only come from experience – made it necessary for me to make the point; 'prison as it stands generally dehuman-izes,' I said, 'but this place is designed to rehumanise'. The tour over (and) as they walked back to the boardroom . . . I recalled my reaction to the welcoming handshake I received from the prison probation officer soon after I arrived. For days after-wards, my eyes welled up every time I remembered it. (James 2002)

From this brief review it is clear that the voluntary sector has had an almost constant part to play during the twentieth century, but that as identity politics took hold in the middle of the last century it became necessary to rethink the style of delivery. The traditional definition of 'voluntary' – of the privileged working out of a sense of altruism, com-passion or their faith for the less privileged – created dependence. It had never been an equal or empowering way of working, and by the end of the century had become increasingly unacceptable. Peter Walker, Minister of Environment in 1969, presented a report to an international conference of Habitat in Sweden entitled '50 million Vol-unteers'. The report was based on the assumption that the nature of volunteering was changing; it was no longer confined to a minority but was becoming the natural means by which people were becoming involved in the life of their community. The voluntary sector was proving to have a distinctive role in enabling and empowering people to become citizens. However, Peter Walker certainly did not have prisoners in mind in this context. We need to do so and to explore and develop opportunities for volunteering within the prison. This should be a key component of all our work of rehabilitation and resettlement of prisoners.

The challenge facing us as Christian groups working in prisons in the twenty-first century is finally to leave behind the philanthropic paternalism of the Victorians. We need to campaign for that same political shift that has already taken place in attitudes towards women, black and minority communities, people with mental health needs and people with disabilities to occur in society's treatment of, and attitude towards, prisoners.

What is required is nothing less than a change in perception by statutory and voluntary staff and among prisoners themselves – to learn to see prisoners as citizens with skills that can be used for their own benefit and that of other inmates. The very idea might seem revolutionary and fraught with difficulty in an institution which is so 'closed' and 'behind the times'.

The challenge is huge, but one can take comfort from the sector's long and honourable tradition of innovation – from National Childbirth Trust classes to hospices, from Amnesty International campaigns to Citizen Advocacy Schemes for people with learning difficulties, from Victim Support to prison Visitors' Centres. The list is as varied as it is long. The creative and innovative solutions devised by voluntary organizations and their members are almost always rooted in personal experience of the issue and the realization that 'the (traditional) ways things are done' often erect unnecessary barriers to an individual's full participation in the community. We need to begin listening to and consulting prisoners about the unnecessary barriers in the prison system which prevent them from addressing their offending behaviour and gaining the skills and confidence to become citizens and contributing members of society.

To summarize, the voluntary sector is, at its best, a service provider, an enabler of people, an innovator and a change agent – roles which demand commitment, risk-taking, trust and a fearlessness in challenging the *status quo*. To carry out these roles in prisons is particularly challenging, and one needs to look for allies and to invest time and energy in building partnerships and coalitions.

This government is explicit in recognizing the distinctive contribution which the voluntary sector and faith communities can make. The White Paper, *Our Towns and Cities: The Future* (DETR 2000) made this clear: 'Faith communities are a distinctive part of the voluntary and community sector. To realise their potential contribution to renewal and social inclusion is a challenging agenda both for faith communities and for other stakeholders.'

We need to build on this commitment, but always to safeguard our freedom and independence; otherwise we will be inhibited from being the change agent and the critic of services which fall short of our ideals.

As Christians we believe that 'God created man in his own image, in the image of God he created him; male and female he created them' (Genesis 1.27, NIV) and that we are to live according to Jesus's response to the question, 'Lord, when did we see you hungry or thirsty or a stranger or needing clothes or sick or in prison, and did not help you?' '. . . whatever you did not do for one of the least of these, you did not do for me' (Matthew 25.44–5, NIV). We believe that every man, woman and child is created in the image of God, that there is the offer of redemption for everyone, whatever the crime, and that everyone has potential and God-given talents and skills. We know from the parable of the talents (Matthew 25.14–30, NIV) we are to do everything in our power to use our talents and to enable others to find and use theirs. In all our practice with prisoners in custody, in our dealings with prison officers, in our work of resettlement with prisoners' families in the community, in schools, in parishes, whether as professional worker, volunteer or parishioner, we need to treat people with decency, with courtesy and as fellow citizens.

It will not be enough for us as volunteers and members of voluntary organizations to work for the right of prisoners to be treated as citizens. In a culture where people are defined as 'rubbish', it requires a high level of commitment and strength to continue believing in the potential of the individual. The negativity is infectious; it affects the way prisoners see themselves and undermines the potential for rehabilitation and reinforces offending behaviour patterns. Opportunities need to be created to give prisoners a sense of self-worth, to learn new skills and to use them for the benefit of themselves and for others.

There are examples of good practice. Inside Out Trust was founded in 1993 'to fund and support activities which provide prison inmates and other offenders and ex-offenders with the knowledge and skills . . .

which are likely to contribute to their reintegration into the community and specifically lead to employment'. The charity trains prisoners to restore bicycles, wheelchairs and computers to export to the developing world; it also has a programme of brailling books for blind people. They work in more than 70 prisons and have provided training and skills for nearly 1,000 prisoners since 1994.

Prisoners' Education Trust provides funding for prisoners to undertake Distance Learning. A grant from them enabled a prisoner to gain an Advance Certificate in Overseas Trade with excellent grades. During the course of his studies he was moved five times to different prisons. He wrote to the Trust:

> This evening it is giving me a great deal of pleasure to be able to write to you and enclose my final pass certificate. It must be two and a half years now since I first applied to you for funding for this qualification. Since then I have taken four exams of three hours each and completed almost 50 TMAs (tutor marked assessments).

This prisoner was also working in the maths room tutoring other prisoners.

In HMP Dovegate, one of the privately managed prisons, the Education Department is using able students as tutors, boosting their self-worth, while expanding educational access for the less able. This sensible and efficient use of prisoners' time should be standard practice throughout the prison estate.

The Listeners Scheme, where prisoners are trained by Samaritans to listen and provide confidential emotional support to other prisoners, is an excellent example of prisoners gaining skills and self-esteem in providing support to their peers.

Nacro and Prison Reform Trust provide voluntary and paid work placements for offenders and ex-offenders. APEX Trust works to support ex-offenders in finding employment. Women inmates in HMP East Sutton Park have set up VISION to provide an advice and information service for the other inmates.

In HMP Holloway, Prison Advice & Care Trust (PACT) collaborated with the Befrienders (that prison's name for the Listener Scheme) to set up 'First Night in Custody'. The aim of the project is to provide support for women entering prison for the first time. The Befrienders already provide invaluable support for distressed women (not first-time prisoners) in Reception. The intention is to develop this partnership, to include the Befrienders in all PACT's training and also to use them as trainers. Research undertaken by the Centre for Crime & Justice Studies, King's College, London into the 'First Night' project included interviews with recipients of the service. One of the common themes identified was that a 'central comforting factor, other than The Bourne Trust (now PACT), is comfort from other women, either cellmates, other inmates or befrienders'. This resource should be recognized, formalized and built on in development of other services supporting new and first-time inmates.

Prison Advice & Care Trust is employing the services of a prisoner who is studying for a Diploma in Photography at the London School of Printing while in an Open Prison. He has taken all the photographs for their newsletter launching the merged charity. He will be paid for his services and recommended to other charities.

The St Giles Trust at HMP Wandsworth is planning to employ two Development Workers to work in partnership with prison staff to recruit, train and manage a team of prisoners to advise other prisoners on housing, education, training and employment before and after release.

The Prison Reform Trust produced *Barred Citizens: Volunteering and Active Citizenship by Prisoners* (2002) which looked at examples of good practice in using prisoners to support one another and questioned why such practice could be followed in some high security prisons but was not happening in prisons of a lower security rating.

These are just some examples of good practice. There are many others, but they are not the norm. They should be replicated throughout the estate and new ways of working introduced to create opportunities for prisoners to take responsibility. But we will encounter considerable opposition to new initiatives. With inadequate staffing levels, prison officers are already overstretched and find themselves bombarded with a proliferation of performance indicators and targets; why should they go out of their way to help 'do-gooders'?

David Ramsbotham, the previous HM Inspector of Prisons, argued for the introduction of the concept of a 'healthy prison'. One applauded the principle but, given the current state of the service, a 'healthy prison' seems a contradiction in terms. The World Health

Organization (WHO Regional Office for Europe) Health in Prisons Project says in its Consensus Statement, '[We are] aware that, in the absence of counter measures, deprivation of freedom is intrinsically bad for mental health and that imprisonment has the potential to cause significant mental harm.'

They go on to say: 'Mental health . . . requires an underlying belief in our own and others' dignity and worth . . . prison should provide an opportunity for prisoners to be helped towards a sense of the opportunities available to them for personal development . . . in order for this to happen, prisoners must (i) feel safe, (ii) [have] insight into their own offending behaviour, (iii) be treated with positive expectations and respect.'

As Owers' report on HMP Dartmoor showed, and as Judy Clements found, prisoners are routinely treated with disrespect and referred to as 'scum' and 'rubbish'. These attitudes are detrimental to mental health.

The WHO report recommends 'Positive Steps to Mental Well-Being'; two of the steps are: 'Be a friend. You could be a good friend to others too' and 'Get involved. Getting involved or trying something new can help defeat boredom.'

The Manic Depression Fellowship, MIND, Hearing Voices and Depression Alliance all run self-help groups in the community where people with the same diagnosis come together for support and friendship. They have expert knowledge and personal experience of the side-effects of their prescribed medication, they share tried and tested strategies in managing their 'highs', their 'lows', their suicidal thoughts and their vulnerability to self-harm. To suggest that such self-help groups be set up in prison might be thought a radical step too far, but one needs to consider the possibility; the resource implications would be minimal, the value to the individual prisoner in learning to recognize and understand their mood swings and to develop strategies to manage them would be of long-term benefit in prison and back in the community. In Holloway the Befrienders provide confidential support for prisoners experiencing stress, anxiety and panic attacks, all of which are symptoms of mental ill-health. One needs to develop this work and train these volunteers in mental health topics. One could arrange training workshops run by external self-help groups and begin developing relationships that could support the prisoner on release.

All the examples of good practice cited above have in common the involvement and consultation of prisoners. It is disappointing to note that *Shared Responsibilities: Education for Prisoners at a Time of Change,* a study for NATFHE and the Association of Colleges (Braggins 2001) did not consult any prisoners. It aimed to gather an overview of the perceptions of prison governors, education managers and contractors on the state of prison education in England and Wales. Ironically, a study (of the delivery of adult education services) entitled *Shared Responsibilities* did not consult the recipients of the services, let alone consider any responsibilities prisoners themselves could take in delivery of the service. In the 54- page report there was a single reference to peer education. Such serious oversight shows how far we have to travel towards a recognition of the citizenship of prisoners.

The Report found there was difficulty in ensuring that student records moved with prisoners when they were transferred. 'Is there', the Report asked, 'an adequate system for transferring student records when prisoners are transferred to or from your establishment?' Seventy-two per cent said yes, 21 per cent said no. Sixty-seven per cent said they received students' reports irregularly. If the institutional performance is so low, why not consider giving the individual student responsibility for transferring his or her own records? That system would certainly ensure that the committed serious student would not be disadvantaged by the inefficiency of the system. With low levels of literacy and numeracy among the large majority of the prison population, one should provide training for the more able prisoner to mentor and tutor the less able, and one could pay them for this work. It should be standard practice that all able students throughout the estate be involved in the work, and they could be given incentives to participate.

Stephen Pryor's report (Pryor 2001) is as encouraging as *Shared Responsibilities* is discouraging. His 'basic premise is that people offend more easily the worse the opinion they hold of themselves, and the agencies which deal with them only make it worse if they then treat them badly'. He recommends a rethinking of current prison management practice; why in some prisons are prisoners allowed freedom of movement, while in other establishments with the same security rating they are accompanied by prison officers at all times? Education departments, voluntary projects and other services regularly face the frustration of not being able to access prisoners because of a lack of staff: should it not be possible to give some prisoners the responsibility of moving around the prison without escort? We need to remember that if 'power corrupts and absolute power corrupts absolutely', the reverse – the lack of power – is highly damaging too. When people feel completely powerless and when they feel they have no stake at all in society they are extremely dangerous.

In an already overcrowded and rapidly growing prison population, where even the basis decencies of 'Please', 'Thank you' and a handshake are not part of day-to-day practice, and disrespect is endemic, the likelihood of prisoners being recognized as citizens, as people who can develop their potential and also help other prisoners while in custody, seems slight.

Yet the scale of the task has never discouraged voluntary activists and should not discourage us at the beginning of a new century. We will leave the last word to a Lifer and Listener who worked with Pryor. It is a question all of us working in prisons need to ask ourselves: 'Are we making the best use of the time and people in prison for their futures and the futures of those in the wider community to which they will return?'

As voluntary organizations, as Christian groups, as individuals working with prisoners and their families, we need to work so that we can answer that question with a confident 'Yes.'

References

Beveridge, W. H., *Voluntary Action: A Report on Methods of Social Advance*. George Allen & Unwin, London, 1948.

Braggins, Julia, *Shared Responsibilities: Education for Prisoners at a Time of Change*. NATFHE, 2001.

Clements, Judy, quoted in 'The race we must not lose', *Prison Service News*, September 2000. Available on <www.hmprisons.gov.uk/library>.

DETR, *Our Towns and Cities*, White Paper. 2000.

Farrant, Finola and Levenson, Joe, *Barred Citizens: Volunteering and Active Citizenship by Prisoners*. Prison Reform Trust, London, 2002.

James, Erwin, 'A life inside', *Guardian*, February 2002. Available on <www.guardian.co.uk>.

Levenson, Joe, *Prisoners and the Democratic Process*. Prison Reform Trust Briefing Paper, London, 1998.

Low, Colin, National Federation of the Blind.

Pryor, Stephen, *The Responsible Prisoner: An Exploration of the Extent to which Imprisonment Removes Responsibility Unnecessarily and an Invitation to Change*. Home Office, London, 2001.

10 | Racial Justice in Prisons: Where Are We Now?

Paul Cavadino and May El Komy

ONE OF BISHOP BOB HARDY'S achievements as Bishop for Prisons was to help push the issue of racial justice in prisons up the agenda of both the Prison Service and the churches. This chapter looks at the background to concern over this issue, summarizes the findings of a key Nacro report published in 2000, and assesses the action taken by the Prison Service to promote racial justice since then.

The background

The disproportionate number of prisoners from minority ethnic groups is well known. In June 1999, prisoners from minority groups accounted for 19 per cent of the total prison population (12.3 per cent black, 3 per cent Asian and 3.4 per cent other), 18 per cent of the male prison population (12 per cent black, 12 per cent Asian and 3 per cent other), and 25 per cent of the female prison population (19 per cent black, 1 per cent Asian and 5 per cent other).

Since the Prison Service first began to monitor the ethnicity of prisoners, there has been a similar pattern: minority prisoners were 17 per cent of the prison population in 1985, 16 per cent between 1989 and 1994, 17 per cent in 1995, and 18 per cent between 1996 and 1998.

The Prison Service has taken official steps to respond to the needs of a diverse population for longer than any other criminal justice agency. For example, it was among the first to collect and make public ethnic monitoring statistics, it issued its first instruction to governors on race relations in 1981, and over the years it has taken a series of other initiatives on race relations culminating in the launch of a new streamlined policy on race relations issued as Prison Service Order 2800 in 1997. This said:

> The Prison Service is committed to racial equality. Improper discrimination on the basis of colour, race, nationality, ethnic or national origins, or religion is unacceptable, as is any racially abusive or insulting language or behaviour on the part of any member of staff, prisoner or visitor, and neither will be tolerated.[1]

The order included a set of standards, each with a list of mandatory steps and further recommended actions. The standards cover:

- Legal obligations and Prison Service policy.
- Management structures and performance assessment.
- Ethnic monitoring.
- Facilities and services.
- Complaints and racist incidents.
- External contacts.
- Training and information.

Also in 1997, the then Director General of the Prison Service, Richard Tilt, stressed his commitment to ensuring race equality in prisons at the first-ever national conference of Black Prisoner Support Groups and announced the establishment of a new national race relations policy advisory group, now known as the Director General's Advisory Group on Race.

Two years later, a new Prison Service programme, RESPOND (Race Equality for Staff and Prisoners), was launched with five key objectives:

1 Confront racial harassment and discrimination.
2 Ensure fairness in recruitment, appraisal, promotion and selection.
3 Developing and supporting minority ethnic staff.
4 Ensuring equal opportunities for minority ethnic prisoners.
5 Recruit ethnic minority staff.

Judy Clements OBE was appointed as Race Equality Adviser to give day-to-day leadership to the programme.

The Nacro study

In 1998 the Prison Service commissioned Nacro to conduct a survey of race relations in prisons. The aim was to find out what progress had been made and how much remained to be done, so that the results could provide some signposts for implementing Prison Service Order 2800. Staff and prisoners from all ethnic groups were invited to take part in the survey to express their views on race relations in their prisons. Two women's prisons, four men's prisons and three young offender institutions were involved in the survey.

The survey was conducted using short tick-box questionnaires. Workshops and discussion groups were also held, allowing prisoners and staff to expand on the topics covered in the questionnaire.

The survey respondents consisted of 295 prison employees and 1,223 prisoners. Of the respondent prisoners, 18 per cent were held on remand, 19 per cent were women, and about a third of the sample were male prisoners held in young offender institutions. Sixty-seven per cent of the prisoners in the sample were white, 24 per cent were black, 4 per cent were Asian, 4 per cent described themselves as being of another ethnic origin, and 1 per cent did not answer.

The survey followed two earlier studies of relevance to race relations in prison. The National Prison Survey,[2] conducted in 1991 by the Home Office, aimed to gather information about the background characteristics of prisoners, their perceptions of regimes, and their attitudes to crime and offending. The survey found that white prisoners were more likely than black or Asian prisoners to have left school before 16 and to have truanted before the age of 11. In addition, 44 per cent of white prisoners had no qualifications compared with 30 per cent of black and 40 per cent of Asian prisoners, and just before imprisonment, more minority ethnic prisoners than white prisoners had been working. The survey found a greater interest in education and training among minority prisoners than white prisoners.

Black prisoners were the least likely of all the groups to feel they were well treated by the prison staff. A higher proportion of Asian than either black or white prisoners in the sample said they were assaulted in the last six months, and 14 per cent of minority prisoners said they felt threatened by racist prisoners.

In 1995, the Commission for Racial Equality and the Prison Service published a joint research on race relations in seven prisons.[3] The study found that although Race Relations Management Teams (RRMT) were in place, there were variations in how often they met and in their effectiveness. Additionally, ethnic monitoring systems were in place, but were not always used effectively.

The study also found that communicating race relations policy to staff and prisoners had a low profile and that links with outside organizations such as race relations equality councils were weak and *ad hoc*. There was a very low reporting rate of racist incidents and a lack of effective responses. The study concluded: 'there has been sometimes impressive but uneven progress in establishments since the publication of the Race Relations Manual in 1991 . . . However, there was little appreciation of the need to move to regimes which positively promote racial equality.'

The Nacro survey was undertaken in the light of these findings to look more closely at the perceptions of staff and prisoners in the following key areas:

- Awareness of race relations policy.
- Training.
- The prison regime and facilities.
- Relationships in prisons.
- Racist incidents.
- Community ties.

Prison staff

The majority of the sample (67 per cent) were prison officer grades. The others included administrative workers, governor grades and cleaning and catering staff; educational tutors and lecturers; librarians and health care staff.

Knowledge of race relations policy

The majority of staff (63 per cent) were aware of the new Race Relations Order, yet most (78 per cent) had not received any relevant training. Black staff were less likely to be aware of the new order and were less likely to have received any training on the new order when compared with white staff.

Views on the new Race Relations Order

Staff views varied. It was clear that many staff had not seen it. Comments included: 'Could be another waste of paper. The money could be better spent on a good pay rise'; 'Over-reaction to the Stephen Lawrence Inquiry.'

Race relations training

Of those prison officers and governors posts answering a question on training, 70 per cent said they had received race relations training as new officers. Forty-two per cent said they had received race relations training as serving officers. Only 20 per cent of black staff said this. Black staff were, however, more likely to say that it was useful (30 per cent compared with 19 per cent of white staff).

Ethnic monitoring

The Race Relations Order set out detailed instructions about which areas of prison life should be subject to ethnic monitoring. There were significant ethnic differences in the responses to the question which asked whether staff thought ethnic monitoring was essential; important; a bit useful; or a waste of time. More black staff said that it was essential or important compared with white staff. Of the 22 members of staff who said that it was a waste of time, 21 were white.

Some of the comments on monitoring stressed the need to make use of the results to improve the Prison Service's approach: 'It is vital that it serves as a springboard and helps in a way to stamp out or alleviate the racial problem.' Other responses were more negative: 'Too much paperwork.'

Facilities for minority prisoners

Sixty per cent of black staff knew how to contact outside faith organizations compared with 42 per cent of white staff; 55 per cent of black staff knew how to contact a local Race Equality Council compared with 27 per cent of white staff and 40 per cent of black staff knew how to contact a local community group compared with 26 per cent of white staff.

There was little ethnic variation in responses to questions on whether staff knew how to get hold of minority newspapers and books or special items for the canteen shop such as black skin or hair products. Unsurprisingly, staff in rural or isolated prisons with fewer minority prisoners were less likely to be able to meet these requests.

More black compared with white staff knew how to contact local faith institutions, RECs and local community groups.

Relationships in prison

Staff had a more positive view of staff and prisoner relations than they did of the relations between prisoners of different minority groups. Black staff were less likely than white staff to describe prisoner and officer relations as good or very good, and more likely to rate them as OK.

Physical and verbal abuse

Only eight staff, who were white, said that they had been physically assaulted because of their racial or ethnic origin. All said that this was by prisoners.

Eighty-two staff said they had been subject to verbal abuse because of their ethnic or racial origin. Seventy-two were white, eight were black and two were from 'other' ethnic groups. The majority of staff said that prisoners were responsible for the abuse; visitors were mentioned 12 times and other staff seven times.

Race relations in general

On being asked to assess race relations in their prison on a five-point scale, 12 per cent answered very good; 47 per cent answered OK; 33 per cent said poor; none answered very poor and three did not answer.

Over half the staff said race relations was important in their every day work and a further third said it was important to some extent.

General comments

Sixty-four of the 69 staff who made general comments were white and four were black. The more positive comments acknowledged the importance of race relations, better awareness and information about diversity, and the need for a diverse staff to deal with a diverse prison population. Some comments were also honest about the fact that there are racist attitudes within the Service which need to be tackled. Lack of time and resources to do the job properly was also mentioned by several staff.

The majority of the comments suggested a strong element of denial of any problem or need for action. Many people referred to alleged 'political correctness' and suggested that prisoners used race issues to get what they wanted from the system. A small number of comments revealed a deep form of racism and a lack of understanding for the harm that it does: 'It is a fact that in this area of England there are more blacks committing crimes than whites. No amount of ethnic monitoring can alter that.'

The report of the study recommended that:

- Awareness of Prison Service race relations policy needs to be increased among all staff.
- All staff should receive training in race and equality which is regularly updated.
- The Prison Service needs to do more to explain the value of ethnic monitoring to its staff, to provide feedback and information to them about the results, and to make practical use of the results.
- Staff need to be given more information and guidance on making outside community contacts which benefit prisoners during their sentence and in preparation for release.
- Black staff associations should be formed at all prisons, and a network of support groups established nationally.

Prison life: facilities

It is Prison Service policy that suitable diets, items in the prison shop, religious services and newspapers and books should be provided for ethnic groups. The questionnaire asked about prisoners' experiences of these facilities.

Knowledge of policy

Seventy-three per cent of prisoners said they knew that the Prison Service had a race relations policy, although far fewer knew what the policy actually said. A smaller proportion of minority prisoners knew about the policy. Women were most likely to know about the policy, but fewer minority women were likely to know about the policy.

Only 22 per cent of respondents wrote in who they thought was responsible for race relations in the prison. These answers varied with 62 per cent saying staff, 19 per cent said everybody and 4 per cent saying nobody.

Regimes and facilities

The questionnaire asked whether prisoners were satisfied with 13 areas of prison life.

Variety of prison food

On average, more white prisoners (43 per cent) were satisfied with the food. Black and Asian prisoners were less likely to be satisfied with the food (both 31 per cent) despite several white prisoners complaining that those on special dietary needs such as Muslims got better food than they did.

Goods in the canteen, or prison shop

The results here confirmed that it had often been difficult for black prisoners to get the skincare and hair products that they needed. Black and 'other' minority prisoners were the most dissatisfied with the range of goods available in the prison canteen.

Religious services

Black prisoners were less satisfied than other groups with religious services in the prison, although in general, prisoners showed a fairly high level of satisfaction with this aspect of prison life.

Access to prison work

Asian prisoners were happiest about their access to work and black prisoners were least pleased. Black women were more pleased with this aspect of prison life than white women.

Access to education

Prisoners from all minority groups seemed more pleased than the white group with their access to education. These results were in line with those from the 1991 National Prison Survey which found that minority prisoners have a strong interest in education.

Access to legal advice

Black prisoners expressed the most dissatisfaction here, with only 46 per cent saying they were satisfied compared with 55 per cent white, 55 per cent Asian and 50 per cent of the 'other' group.

Advice about release plans
Black prisoners and those in the 'other' ethnic group were much less satisfied with advice about release (35 per cent and 28 per cent respectively) compared with white and Asian prisoners (48 per cent and 57 per cent). Forty-four per cent of white women expressed satisfaction here compared with 36 per cent of black women.

Personal officer scheme
Asian prisoners were the most satisfied with the personal officer scheme, and prisoners in the 'other' category and black prisoners the least satisfied.

Advice about drug or alcohol misuse
Black and 'other' prisoners were the least pleased here and Asian prisoners were the most satisfied of all the groups.

Access to Samaritans or counselling
Prisoners from all minority groups were less satisfied than the white prisoners here.

Visiting arrangements
All minority prisoners were less satisfied on this point. This could be *partially* accounted for by the high proportion of prisoners from outside the UK held at some of the prisons in the survey.

What else should be provided?
The suggestions from over 300 prisoners who wrote in the space provided included:

- Better food.
- More goods in the canteen.
- Electricity and televisions in cells.
- More gym, more association and more time out of cells.
- Access to showers and clean clothes and bed linen.
- Longer visits, improved facilities for visitors and closer contact with children.

There was a strong demand in one prison with a high foreign national population for a specialist foreign national officer and for people from outside the UK to be treated in the same way as British prisoners.

Overall, the results from this section reflect a generally lower level of satisfaction among minority prisoners, with a few exceptions, notably education.

The report of the survey recommended that:

- The Prison Service needs to do more to make prisoners better informed of its race relations policy, perhaps by introducing a 'plain English' shorter version, or through a video which could be shown to all prisoners as part of their induction to the prison.
- The Prison Service should make more use of ethnic monitoring, surveys, and discussions with prisoners from all groups in order to improve equality of access to prison facilities.

Prison life: relationships

Prisoner–officer relations by ethnic origin

Fewer minority prisoners assessed relations between prisoners and officers as very good or good. Only 165 of the black prisoners said they were good, compared with 25 per cent of the white group. A higher proportion of prisoners in the black and 'other' group described relations as poor or very poor. Black women however assessed prison–officer relations more positively than white women, with 37 per cent saying they were very good or good, compared with 33 per cent.

Racial incidents

A 1994 research study on racist incidents in prisons[4] had found that more Asian prisoners described themselves as victims of racial incidents between prisoners, with one third saying they had been victimized, on average, five times in the previous three months. A quarter of black prisoners said they had been victimized by other prisoners on average four times. Nearly half the black prisoners, a third of Asian prisoners and a quarter of those in the 'other' group said that they had been racially victimized by staff. Verbal abuse was the most common form of racial incident and the most common form of complaint by black and Asian prisoners. The main reason that prisoners gave for not reporting incidents was that they believed 'nothing would be gained by complaining'.

The Nacro survey asked prisoners about their experiences in the light of these findings.

Physical assaults

Twelve per cent of black and Asian prisoners said that they had been physically assaulted, as did 8 per cent of the 'other' group but only 4 per cent of white prisoners. Of the 82 prisoners who said they had been the victim of physical abuse because of their racial or ethnic origin, 34 said staff had been involved.

Verbal abuse

Forty-nine per cent of the Asian prisoners said they had been verbally abused, as did 27 per cent of black prisoners, 22 per cent of the 'other' prisoners and 13 per cent of the white prisoners. Other prisoners were mentioned as being responsible by 112 prisoners, and staff were mentioned by 87 prisoners.

Reporting incidents

Only 7 per cent said that they had reported incidents. By ethnic group the figures were 3 per cent white, 8 per cent Asian, 13 per cent of those in the 'other' ethnic group and 18 per cent of black prisoners. Most people who had reported incidents said that nothing had happened, or that they were 'still waiting'. As with the 1994 research, the main reasons given for not reporting incidents included feelings that nothing would be achieved and fear of reprisals and the desire not to be seen as a grass. Some prisoners also mentioned bureaucracy and the length of time it would take as a deterrent.

The report of the survey recommended that:

- High priority must be given to reducing the under-reporting of racist incidents, and to tackle the lack of confidence in the fairness of the system.
- A real effort must be made to tackle racism in prisons, not only by using the formal complaints procedures but also by a programme of education for all who live and work behind the walls.
- The Prison Service should ensure it will be able to comply with the 1998 Human Rights Act, to ensure none of its own staff are infringing the human rights of prisoners or colleagues, and to protect all in prison from violations of their human rights.

Prisoners and community links

Prisoners were asked whether they had contact with outside religious or faith institutions, local community groups, and community groups in their home areas. Over a third of black prisoners and half of Asian prisoners said they were in contact with outside faith organizations. Eight per cent of all respondents had contact with a local community group, and with community groups in their home areas.

Table 10.1 shows the number and percentages of prisoners saying they received regular visits from family and friends.

Table 10.1: Prisoners receiving regular visits from family and friends

Regular visits from	White	Black	Asian	Other
Spouse/partner	324 (40%)	113 (38%)	18 (35%)	18 (39%)
Children	169 (21%)	55 (22%)	6 (12%)	8 (17%)
Other family members	433 (53%)	139 (47%)	38 (75%)	24 (52%)
Friends	364 (47%)	133 (45%)	26 (51%)	16 (35%)

There were particular ethnic differences in the replies of women prisoners in relation to visits. Thirty per cent of white women received regular visits form partners/spouses compared with 15 per cent of black women, and 28 per cent of white women were visited by children compared with 15 per cent of black women.

The report recommended that:

- The Prison Service should make it mandatory for prisons to invite representatives of community groups to join the RRMT.
- The Prison Service should undertake further research into the different responses from women shown in the survey, to assess the impact of imprisonment on family and community ties in different communities.

Prisoners: general perceptions

The final question in the survey asked prisoners to describe race relations on a five-point scale. There was also room to write in comments, which one in four respondents made use of. Some seminar or discussion groups were also held to supplement the information gathered from the questionnaire.

General assessment of race relations

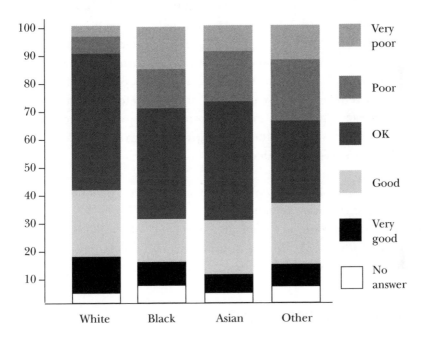

Figure 10.1: Perceptions of race relations

Prisoners from all minority groups were less likely to assess race relations as very good or good, and more likely to say they were poor or very poor. Thirty-six per cent of black women said that race relations were very poor or poor compared with 22 per cent of white women.

One third of black respondents and 44 per cent of respondents in the 'other' group wrote in comments compared with 21 per cent of white and 28 per cent of Asian prisoners. Attitudes among white prisoners varied. Some felt resentful and commented that too much was done for black and Asian prisoners to the detriment of white prisoners: 'There should be an independent body for white people. There is nothing for us.'

Other white prisoners seemed to want to avoid trouble and confrontation of any sort and said that they did not see a problem. A third group of white prisoners – the smallest number of comments – felt that black and Asian prisoners were picked on and did not receive fair treatment: 'The screws are racist bastards, especially to the Asians.'

Comments from black prisoners in the main pointed to the racism they experienced in prison from both staff and other prisoners: 'Prison officers think we are all dogs and a few have told us to our faces.' 'I believe there is an underlying tone of racism in this prison that is not too prevalent but nevertheless is subtle and enough to make one, as a minority prisoner, feel a little uncomfortable at times.' Comments from Asian prisoners reflected similar concerns and also referred to verbal and other abuse: 'There's no minority community prison officer in this prison who can support minority groups' problems in or outside.'

The report recommended that:

- The mismatch of perceptions between staff and prisoners needs to be explored in more detail.
- Ways must be found to give prisoners more of a voice, by providing more formal and informal avenues through which they can express opinions about prison matters.

What has happened since?

The report concluded that the Prison Service's message on race equality – its policy, its RESPOND programme, its high-level public commitment – was not yet getting through. Policy was not understood, and training – where it was given at all – did not equip staff to deal fairly with each other or with those in their charge on the day-to-day basis. In addition, many staff were quite happy to leave race relation issues to the Race Relations Liaison Officers and not take any personal responsibility for providing non-discriminatory regimes. Racist incidents were just as commonplace as they ever were and just as rarely reported or acted upon. Prisoners' sense of pointlessness and powerlessness rang out from these results.

Since the Nacro survey was published, the Prison Service has taken a series of further steps to promote race equality in line with a number of the report's recommendations. For example:

- In the first year of the RESPOND programme, recruitment and selection training courses were revised, considerably enhancing the elements of race awareness in selection processes. Two years on there are signs of improvement, such as the number of minority ethnic candidates succeeding in securing places on the Service's accelerated promotion schemes (10 per cent and 9 per cent in 2000 and 2001 respectively).
- A new Chaplain General, the Venerable William Noblett, was appointed with a multi-faith remit supported by the Muslim Adviser, Maqsood Ahmed.
- In 2001 the RESPECT (Race Equality for Staff) Prison Service minority ethnic staff support network was launched nationally, with the aim of eliminating racism in the workplace. It has over 1,700 members and offers services to the victims of racism, including a freephone support line staffed by specially trained volunteers.
- Four new racially aggravated offences have been introduced into the Prison Discipline Manual and can now be separately monitored. The Staff Code of Conduct and Discipline is to be strengthened to include racially motivated offences and to emphasize that racial harassment and discrimination and racially motivated convictions constitute gross misconduct. With the support of the Prison Officers' Association, the Director General has announced that any staff member found to be a member of the National Front, the British National Party or Combat 18 will be dismissed.
- The prisoner complaint form has been revised to include a tick-box on the front where complainants can indicate if they believe their complaint involves a racial element. A pilot is under way of a revised racist incident reporting form to make it easier for any third party within prison to report a racist incident. A standardized log is being piloted to record all racist incidents, and this log must be presented to the Race Relations Management Team at every meeting.
- The Service has designed new diversity training which places an emphasis on race issues and has trained Prison Service trainers to deliver this training. The entry level training programme for prison

officers includes specific race relations sessions, and instruction in drill has been abolished in order to increase the amount of time spent on race awareness issues.

• Under the leadership of the Race Equality Adviser, the Service has created a Diversity and Equality Group. This is drawing up a Race Equality Scheme and action plan to achieve full compliance with the Race Relations (Amendment) Act 2000.

While an enormous amount remains to be done to combat racism and promote race equality across the Prison Service, there is now an unprecedented mood of determination to eradicate racism from the Service – a determination which owes much to the strong personal commitment of the Director General, Martin Narey. If this is to be translated into reality on prison landings throughout the country, staff are the key. All the skin and hair products that can be jammed on shelves and all the multicultural open days in the calendar year will not help if staff do not understand and ensure fundamental human rights – including freedom from the fear of assault because of racial origin or religious belief, freedom from discrimination, freedom from cruel, inhumane and degrading treatment, and the right to dignity and respect. The struggle against racism in prisons will only be won when every staff member understands and accepts his or her duty to ensure and to protect these fundamental freedoms for every prisoner and every member of staff.

Notes

1   Prison Service Order 2800: Race Relations. Home Office 1997.
2   Walmsley, Roy and others, *The National Prison Survey 1991: Main Findings.* Home Office Research Study 128. HMSO, London, 1992.
3   'The Management of Race Relations in Prison Establishments'. CRE/ Prison Service, London, 1995.
4   Burnett, Ros and Farrell, Graham, *Reported and Unreported Racial Incidents in Prisons.* Centre for Criminological Research, University of Oxford, Occasional Paper No. 14, 1994.

11 | Release from Custody: What are the Risks?

John Harding

Introduction

Each year, about 90,000 adult prisoners and young offenders under the age of 21 are released from custody; some of them (the more serious and dangerous offenders) will be supervised under strict licence requirements by the Probation Service, but the majority, especially those serving a period of less than 12 months in prison, will be unsupervised, although they have an option to seek help and assistance from the local probation area on a voluntary basis. Most prisoners, as they leave the prison gate – despite what steps may have been taken to prepare for their resettlement on the outside through attendance on offending behaviour programmes, remedial education or, if available, vocational skills training – face an uncertain future. Only a minority will return to a stable domestic situation where they continue to enjoy the benefits of family support and a network of reliable friends. The majority will have to fend for themselves, find accommodation, look for work or entry to a government-sponsored training scheme, initially rely on a prison discharge grant or income support, and stay out of trouble, if they are to avoid a swift return to the courts and prison. For some – particularly those whose offending was triggered by drug or alcohol misuse – the temptation, despite the availability of drug treatment and counselling in prison and 'walk-in' treatment agencies in the community, to engage, once more, in substance misuse, is irresistible.

Here are the words of a young man in custody about to be released; his fears and uncertainties are palpable:

No, they need to do a lot more after-care. All right you can throw people in prison and say he's got to stop doing it but where's the help to stop doing it? Throwing you back into society, what do they do then? They've got no money, no job, so they are going to take drugs, what can you expect? (Home Office 2000b)

The message from the Home Office study of young people's views of their future was clear in terms of the fear and a high probability of re-offending. Like many of their adult counterparts in prison, they believed it was up to them to stop re-offending, but they needed considerable help from family, friends, prospective employers and prison and probation staff to do so. They also recognized the role of government in helping to create social policies that are inclusive, with access to opportunities designed to stop the cycle of re-offending: employment, supportive accommodation, drug and alcohol treatment, and widely available programmes focused on ways of overcoming specific offending behaviours.

Such a challenge to the government and those responsible for resettlement planning, the prison and probation services and the voluntary sector invites the question of what arrangements are already in place to meet the expectations of offenders awaiting release from custody, and what risks such offenders pose in terms of re-offending and potential harm to the public. In addition, as has already been alluded to, since there are gaps in the span of resettlement coverage for certain less serious prisoners, what plans have the government to strengthen the protection of the public and lessen the possibility of further crimes?

The current arrangements for resettling prisoners

The 1991 Criminal Justice Act introduced the principle of the seamless sentence as 'a wholly new concept, namely that a sentence be served partly in custody and partly in the community with the offender being liable to recall to custody right up to the end of the sentence'. Resettlement began at the point of the sentence, continued through the period of imprisonment and ended up with the completion of the licence. It was defined as 'work embracing all the assistance given to offenders and their families by the prison and probation services and outside agencies and tied in with the training, education and work experience for each inmate'. Risk assessments and confronting offending behaviour were defined as essential elements of the process and identified as the joint responsibility of the prison and probation services. All prisoners serving less than four years would be released automatically halfway through their licence. Those sentenced to less than 12 months would not be subject to any form of licence, but be subject to Automatic Unconditional Licence (AUL). Those who had received sentences of between one and four years would be supervised up to the three-quarter point, remaining liable to recall up to the end of this sentence. This was known as Automatic Conditional Release (ACR). Offenders sentenced to four years and over became eligible for Discretionary Conditional Release (DCR), following a decision by the Parole Board at the halfway point of sentence. If released, they were supervised to the three-quarter point and were liable to recall at the end of this sentence. Offenders not released on parole were released automatically at the two-thirds point and supervised to the three-quarter point in the same way as ACR offenders.

Despite the good intentions which lay behind the Act, a review of practice in 1995 showed that sentence planning was not meeting its stated objectives (Simon and Corbett 1995). Plans were not properly integrated within prison regimes: it was not a meaningful process for staff and prisoners. There was little reference in plans to re-offending and no evidence of joint ownership between prison and probation staff in the whole process.

In July 1997, a Prison/Probation Review was set up to identify options for closer and more integrated work. Although the merger of the two services was considered, this was abandoned in favour of a new National Probation Service with a parallel hierarchy and regional structure to the Prison Service. Several action points arose out of the dialogue between the two services, including the notion of a Joint Accreditation Panel, the inauguration of shared risk and needs assessments for prisoners, and shared use of resources and staff development. The whole process was consolidated in 1999 when the government published the Correctional Policy Framework, which set out for the first time a common structure for the Prison and Probation Services (Home Office 1999a). Its purpose was to ensure the delivery of the common aim of 'effective execution of the sentences of the court so as to reduce re-offending and protect the public'. Within the framework, commitments were agreed to place long-held intentions on a more professional footing; the first of these related to the formation of a Joint Accreditation Panel (JAP) of international and national experts who would approve a range of effective practice programmes which were evidence-based and likely to reduce reconviction rates, whether the programmes were delivered in prison or by the Probation Service in the community.

Effective practice in addressing offending behaviour

Over the past decade a great deal of work with offenders in this country and abroad, particularly in the USA and Canada, has come under the banner of 'what works'. In essence, the approach entails consistent and accurate assessment of the risk of reconviction and harm and the personal factors relevant to re-offending, plus the development of a core curriculum of evidence-based programmes for the use of prison and probation services aimed at changing offending behaviour. Evidence is now available which shows that properly conducted offender treatment programmes can have a significant effect on reconviction rates, whether these programmes are conducted in the prison or in the community. Calculations are based on a range of estimated reconviction effects which suggest that if programmes are well designed and well run, they might reduce reconviction rates by 5 to 15 percentage points.

The Prison Service, by the mid-1990s, had developed two such programmes based on effectiveness criteria for delivery in a limited number of prisons in England and Wales. They were the Sex Offender Treatment Programme (SOTP) and the Enhanced Thinking Skills Programme (ETS). By the late 1990s, the Probation Service similarly embraced effective practice principles, mirroring the earlier work of the Prison Service and extending the range of offence-based programmes (Home Office 1998). The first report of the JAP in 2000, however, emphasized the importance of continuity between both services, particularly in respect of resettlement (Joint Accreditation Panel 2000). It stressed the need for relevant information to be shared so that offenders are properly monitored and supervised, the public protected and victims aided.

Drugs and alcohol

As part of the 'What Works' strategy, the 1998 Comprehensive Spending Review allocated the Prison Service an additional £76 million from 1999 to 2002 to develop a strategy for tackling and treating drug misuse in prison. The scale of the problem is immense, with over 40 per cent of sentenced prisoners experiencing some degree of drug dependence in the year before they went to prison (Ellis and Marshall 1998). In the absence of any action to break these offenders' drug habits, some 8,000 drug-dependent prisoners would be released into the community each year. All prisons now provide counselling, assessment, referral, advice and throughcare services (CARATS), and the number of intensive drug rehabilitation units in prison has doubled since 1997. It is calculated that by 2004 some 25,000 prisoners a year will use CARATS services, with nearly 6,000 entering an intensive rehabilitation programme or therapeutic community. As well as drugs, the Prison Service will deliver a strategy for prisoners where alcohol was a factor in their offending (Home Office 2001b).

For drug-misusing prisoners, despite the promise of the new prisoner initiative, the problems, for some, still remain in the days and weeks after release. A recent survey in 2001 revealed that about half of drug-using prisoners who had been receiving treatment while in custody reported being offered help to obtain treatment on release (Home Office 2000b). However, only 11 per cent had a fixed appointment with a drug agency four months after their release; half were back to using heroin on a daily basis. To strengthen the resolve of prisoners staying off drugs after release, the government, under the terms of the Criminal Justice and Courts Services Act 2000, is piloting drug testing for long-sentence prisoners on licence, serving the final part of their sentence in the community. The measure has two purposes: both as a deterrent, and as a means of identifying offenders who need additional support in the community to avoid re-offending.

By way of extra support to short-term prisoners with a history of drug offending, the government intends to establish a further five hostels, available for men and women at the point of release by 2003. These measures, worthy in themselves, are small scale by comparison to the size of the problem. There needs to be a more comprehensive review of treatment services for drug and alcohol misusers leaving prison, particularly in relation to availability of drug rehabilitation residential units in the community, where joint funding is provided by health trusts and social services departments. Too often, long-term addicts in prison apply for a place in such units on release, and are refused, not on the grounds of their needs, but because of a local or regional shortfall in revenue funding. Similarly, the range of supported, specialist housing for vulnerable, substance-misusing offenders on release, especially in metropolitan areas, is already too small and fragmented to match the volume of need. In this respect, the revenue base underpinning the government's forthcoming Supporting People legislation in 2003 by the DETR needs urgent reappraisal.

Other resettlement issues

Apart from the specialist needs of drug-misusing offenders, we now know much more about prisoners in relation to education, employment and homelessness. For example, an ex-prisoner who is unemployed doubles the chances of reconviction (Simon and Corbett 1995). A homeless ex-offender increases the likelihood of reconviction by two and a half times (Singleton 1998). Almost three fifths of those sent to prison are unemployed when sentenced (Ellis and Marshall 1998) and up to 90 per cent are estimated to leave prison without a job (House of Commons 1991). About a third of prisoners lose their homes while in prison (Singleton 1998) and two fifths will be homeless on release (Home Office 1992). Low educational attainment, truancy and school exclusions are all linked to offending. Forty-five per cent of all male prisoners under 30 have no formal qualifications (compared with less than 10 per cent of the general population between 20 and 30) and about 60 per cent of young prisoners aged 15 to 20 are at or below an NVQ level 1 in reading (Home Office 1999b).

What is to be done? First, as part of a new £30 million Custody to Work programme, young offenders will receive up to 30 hours a week education and vocational skills training in Young Offender Institutions. These arrangements, as with adults, will be co-ordinated by the DfES with the Prison Service. For adult prisoners, the new programme goal aim is to double the number of them going into jobs on release from prison and improve their chances of finding accommodation. The challenge lies in gearing prison industries and workshops to prepare

prisoners more effectively for jobs which match market-place requirements.

The plans laid out in the government's *Criminal Justice: The Way
Ahead* document fail, however, to address one major obstacle: the
growing size of the prison population, which has risen by a further
2,500 places since the General Election in 2001, to approximately
68,500. With an overall shortage in prison places and the inexorable
rise in demand by the courts for the use of prison, regimes suffer, education programmes are cut, and too many prisoners wastefully spend
much more time locked up in their cells with few constructive pursuits.
If Custody to Work is to succeed, the government and the courts, acting
in concert, need to cut back on the use of prison, especially for short-
term property offenders, serving less than 12 months imprisonment
(Home Office 2001b).

Hopefully, the long-awaited findings of the government's Social
Exclusion Unit on the resettlement of prisoners, due to be published in
2002, will further examine the scope for less reliance on prison and
reducing offending by ex-prisoners. Already, the unit is examining a
range of practical issues such as:

- whether the low levels of financial support for prisoners, immediately following release, encourages crime;
- whether more could be done to suspend housing tenancies upon
  imprisonment, to prevent prisoners running up substantial rent
  arrears;
- whether the present lack of compulsory supervision for short-term
  prisoners has contributed to higher levels of re-offending.

Developing risk assessments of prisoners

As part of the work undertaken by the Prison/Probation Review in
1999, the services agreed that they would develop an offender assessment tool, known as OASys, based on research about offence-related
factors. Prior to this declaration, probation officers had relied on a
small number of quite complex assessment instruments which produced a profile of offenders' problems and a calculation of their risk of
offending. Such risk assessments entails both the classification of each
offender into a general risk category (normally low, medium or high

risk) and an appraisal of the specific nature of the risk he or she poses, including the identification of any circumstances which may increase the risk of an offence being committed.

For sex offenders, a Prison Service psychologist, David Thornton, devised a separate assessment tool, known as the Structured Anchored Clinical Judgement (SACJ) which broadly assesses the level of risk that a sex offender will commit another sexual offence.

OASys, which is now at a stage of extensive piloting with some probation areas and prisons, is expected to be fully implemented in paper form by 2003, with a computerized version to follow. When finalized, OASys will be a practical expression of seamlessness between the prison and probation services and police areas, involving the latter forces when plans are made for an offender to be released. The new risk assessment can be used by a probation officer preparing a pre-sentence report for the courts or by a discipline staff member when a prisoner is committed to custody following sentence and reviewed at critical points to determine a person's progress before release.

Like previous risk assessments, the OASys process relies on two separate but related strands of measurement: static risk and dynamic risk. Static risk refers to the risk that offenders represent on the basis of factors that they cannot change, i.e. their previous convictions and offending history and elements of their family history. Dynamic risk factors are those relating to risk that can or could change over a period of time. They include anti-social attitudes, criminal associates, poor decision-making, poor interpersonal skills, few positive role models, drug and alcohol dependence, and little respect for the law.

A dynamic risk assessment also needs to distinguish between the individuals' offending-related needs and prisoners' relevant social circumstances. The latter become particularly relevant in the months before a prisoner's release, and they include social isolation, no work, low income and no accommodation.

The assessment process is predicated on the principle that the protection of the public should always take precedence over needs of the individual in any planned intervention. From the outset, the probation officer or prison staff member uses the assessment process and subsequent supervision plan to engage the offender in changing attitudes and behaviour. The prisoner's response to the assessment will in itself generate evidence so that offence-related needs can be matched to the most suitable accredited offending behaviour programme, be it of a long or short duration. The processes of delivering programmes, managing cases and reintegrating offenders into the community will, in turn, generate more information on risk of dangerousness and re-offending, needs and motivation.

It is often the case that programme work begun in prison with an offender on his/her behaviour requires a parallel intervention by the probation area when the prisoner is released on licence. Thus, a Parole Board panel, having read the risk assessment, and noted the prisoner's response to a particular offence-related programme, may take the recommendation of a reporting home-based probation officer that x participates in a further sex offending treatment programme run by the service from its community offices. As part of the whole dialogue with a prisoner about his or her forthcoming release, the issue of risk and selected interventions that match his or her own needs is openly discussed with prison staff and the probation areas resettlement team. Prisoners are warned before release that failure to comply with a Parole Board licence condition of attendance on a programme could lead to a swift return to prison for the completion of the rest of their sentence.

Constructive prisoner resettlement, as the risk assessment model illustrates, is not just about finding the appropriate programme; it is also concerned to address the social circumstances in which the prisoner finds him- or herself. As we have discovered, many are homeless and most will be unemployed at the point of release: two factors closely associated with re-offending. Although pressure for places on the National Probation Service's 200 hostels is intense, probation officers will endeavour, say, in the case of a longer term prisoner who is homeless and committed a serious offence, to find him a hostel with a condition of residence approved by the Parole Board. Likewise, although jobs cannot be easily secured on release, the probation officer will refer a prisoner to a specialist employment agency with particular skills in assessing and placing ex-prisoners in training and work.

Offenders' careers

In discussing the scale of risk to the public represented by prisoners returning from custody, it is timely to remind ourselves of the general pattern of offending, making distinctions between those offenders whose delinquent behaviour is persistent, and those for whom offending is a transitory process. We know that large numbers of people, particularly male, commit crime at some point in their lives, and a large proportion of the population has at least one criminal conviction. 22 per cent of males and 4 per cent of females currently aged 10 to 45 have a conviction for at least one standard list offence (Prime 2001).

Recent (unpublished) Home Office data based on the Offenders Index suggest the likelihood of there being 1.2 million active offenders in the community, falling into three categories:

- persistent offenders (those with high rates of offending as measured by convictions) and a high likelihood of reconviction: 150,000 males, 5,000 females;
- persistent but lower-rate offenders, i.e. those whose convictions are at a lower rate, spread over time: 336,000 males and 4,000 females;
- short career offenders, those with few convictions and low likelihood of reconviction: 600,000 males and 97,000 females.

The picture presented by all the available data here is one in which offenders, for the most part, fall into two groups: those who desist from crime relatively quickly, on first being cautioned, convicted or sentenced; and those who are undeterred, slower to desist and commit larger numbers of offences over longer periods.

Breaking down the data further, we find that in the population as a whole, the peak age of known offending by males is 18, and this has been so for the past ten years. For females, the peak age is 15. The highest proportion of known offenders in relation to the population at large lies between 15 to 24 years of age.

The nature of persistence

Most persistent offenders, the majority of the prison population, tend to start their careers at an early age, but many early convictions do not result in long careers. Less than 5 per cent of offenders born in 1953 who had a first conviction before the age of 15 had more than 20 convictions before the age of 46. A persistent offender in this context means one who has had at least three previous convictions, and the date for a current offence is within three years of the offender's most recent conviction.

As has already been implied, the most powerful predictor of reconviction is the previous criminal history, but social variables can also be significant. Personal factors such as anti-social attitudes have also been shown to contribute directly to criminal behaviour. The most prevalent social variables are:

- drug misuse is most strongly linked with the likelihood of reconviction;
- problems with employment, accommodation and money are also significant;
- alcohol misuse is significant in relation to older offenders.

The impact of sentencing on crime

Re-conviction rates of offenders provide one of the viable means of assessing the national impact of community and custodial penalties in preventing re-offending. In general, although most offenders desist quickly, persistent offenders, in the majority of cases, had disappointingly high re-conviction rates.

If we compare the re-conviction within two years of the prisoner's discharge from custody or an offender commencing a community penalty, the outcomes are identical: 56 per cent discharged prisoners, 56 per cent of offenders subject to community penalties (Home Office 1999b).

Looking more closely at the custodial figures, we discover variations according to the length of sentence served, the age of the offender and the offence category. Of released prisoners, re-conviction rates are higher for those serving shorter sentences than for those released under longer terms. This is shown by the following rates of reconviction within two years of discharge in 1996:

- 60 per cent (up to 12 months sentence);
- 53 per cent (over 12 months and up to four years);
- 31 per cent (over four years and up to ten years);
- 29 per cent (over ten years, excluding life sentences);
- 5 per cent (life-sentence prisoners).

Young offenders fare much worse in terms of re-conviction. Of males discharged from prison and re-convicted within two years, the figures are as follows:

- 85 per cent (age at sentence 14–16);
- 74 per cent (age at sentence 17–20).

A large proportion of the convictions of discharged prisoners result in re-imprisonment. Of adult males discharged in 1996, 52 per cent of males returned to prison; for females, 45 per cent were similarly re-imprisoned.

There are also variations for offence category. Offenders in prison for some offences are more likely to be re-convicted within two years of discharge, than for others. Of those in prison for burglary and discharged in 1996, 76 per cent were reconvicted within two years. Comparable rates in that year were:

- 71 per cent (theft and burglary);
- 55 per cent (robbery);
- 24 per cent (fraud and forgery);
- 19 per cent (sexual offences).

As we have seen, re-conviction rates are generally lower for prisoners discharged from longer sentences. These changes can be partly explained by the difference in criminal history, sex, age and offence category, as there is a similar fall in the predicted rate, based on these factors. It is also significant that these adult prisoners serving longer sentences are subject to post-release supervision, often in the form of parole, or life sentence licence.

Parole and the life licence release decisions are highly selective. Their approach is governed by the Home Secretary's directions, which state that the primary principle is the protection of the public. A balance has to be maintained between the risk a prisoner might pose through the commission of a further offence, and the benefit both to the offender and the public of early supervised release, which might assist his or her rehabilitation and reduce the risk of re-offending.

Of 5,576 parole applications made in 2000–2001, 46 per cent of applications were granted. In that year, some 9.6 per cent of parolees were recalled to prison for failure to keep in touch with their probation officer, failure to comply with conditions, or further offences. The actual re-offence rate in that year for re-offending on licence remains a low figure of 3.8 per cent. Of life sentence cases in the same year, some 803 cases were considered; 21 per cent of these were granted life licence. Some 2.6 per cent of cases had the life licence revoked, mainly for technical violations.

There is evidence overall that parole, at the very least, delays the onset of re-conviction, and has a net effect, over two years, of reducing the number of times prisoners are re-convicted after release, but it remains to be seen whether this effect persists over a longer follow-up period (Ellis and Marshall 1998).

Conclusions: issues and thoughts

In reviewing the impact of sentencing by the courts on offenders in custody and the risks they pose on release in terms of further re-offending, a number of issues begin to emerge. Younger offenders, particularly those under 21, re-offend at a disproportionate rate to their adult counterparts. The overwhelming majority of these young people are serving less than 12 months, mainly for non-violent offences. Indeed, over a quarter of the males and almost half the females in this group are serving sentences of three months or less. All 18- to 21-year-olds serving less than 12 months receive three months supervision on licence managed by the Probation Service. However, it is arguable whether their practical resettlement needs are being met. Even very short sentences will all too often result in loss of accommodation, employment and family ties. This has a particularly damaging effect for young offenders making the difficult transition from childhood to adulthood. A disproportionate number of those confined at this age will also suffer from mental health problems, a history of self-harm, drug and alcohol abuse and the absence of family support; at least 40 per cent of them come from care background in local authority children's homes. The period of custody, for these short-termers, is of little benefit since there is not sufficient time to address aspects of education or offending behaviour.

Once more, we need to examine the value of such short sentences for this age group and make better use of alternative community-based sentences run by the Probation Service that hold and support young people, rather than disrupt once more the slow and painful process of maturing.

Some of the same reasoning might equally apply to the 60 per cent of the adult prison population who are serving less than 12 months in prison and are not entitled to Statutory After Care. The Halliday Report has recommended that all such sentences should normally consist of a maximum period of three months in custody and the minimum period of six months supervision on release (Home Office 2001b). Many of this group need not be imprisoned, considering the range of community punishments that are now in place, but few would quarrel with the idea that the support and correctional measures available to the more serious offenders should also be applied to the lesser sentenced adult offenders. The use of parole for longer-sentence groups shows some promising evidence of a reductive effect in re-offending; the logic could equally be applied to others.

Much of the thrust of this chapter has described the importance of effective practice programmes matching risk assessment to the individual's offending profile and recording the need for continuity in relation to sentence planning between prison and probation staff. There is, too, no doubting of the government's resolve that the principal public protection agencies – the prisons, Probation Service and the police – try to reduce re-offending by potentially dangerous offenders on release from custody. The Crime and Disorder Act 1998 gave courts the powers to extend supervision periods for sex offenders up to ten years and up to five years for violent offenders. In addition, all sex offenders and potentially dangerous offenders, serving over four years, will be discussed by public protection panels, usually convened by local probation and police senior staff, to manage additional controls for such offenders beyond the supervisory process itself. Such actions might include the use of electronic monitoring, visits to the offender's address and, in extreme cases, the seeking of a Sex Offender Court Order to restrict the offender's movements.

These and other measures are all designed to reduce the risk of harm and re-offending by offenders for the general public. They are not foolproof. The risk assessment can only identify the probability of harm and assess the key impact of individuals and pose a series of interventions which may diminish the risk or reduce harm. Take the example of sex offenders; while the responsible agencies can identify known offenders and protect the public as best they can from 'stranger danger' in the manner described, they can do little to forestall predatory behaviour within a family whereby an undetected offender, be it a father, brother, cousin or uncle, chooses to indecently assault a child. In these and other high-profile cases, averting risk and damage is, therefore, not just the responsibility of the agencies charged with protecting society, but a challenge to all of us, wherever we are, to be more vigilant and alert in confronting unacceptable behaviour in whatever form it takes.

References and Further Reading

Ellis, T., and Marshall, P., 'Does Parole Work?' *Home Office Research* Bulletin 39 (1998), pp. 43–50.

HM Treasury (2000) Prudent for a Purpose: Building Opportunity and Security for All. Spending Review 2000. HM Treasury 2000.

Home Office (1992): *The National Prison Survey 1991: Main Findings.* Home Office 1992.

Home Office (1995): Prison Service Order 2200. 1995.

Home Office (1996): *The Housing Needs of Ex-offenders.* Research Bulletin 78. Home Office 1996.

Home Office (1998): Probation Unit, *Effective Practice Initiative: A National Implementation Plan for the Effective Supervision of Offenders.* Probation Circular 35/1998. Stationery Office 1998.

Home Office (1999a): Correctional Policy Unit, *Protecting the Public: the Correctional Policy Framework: Effective Execution of the Sentences of the Courts so as to Reduce Re-offending and Protect the Public.* Home Office 1999.

Home Office (1999b): *Reconvictions of Offenders Sentenced or Discharged from Prison in 1995, England and Wales.* Statistical Bulletin 19. Home Office 1999.

Home Office (2000a): *Prison Statistics, England and Wales 1999.* Stationery Office 2000.

Home Office (2000b): *The Nature and Effectiveness of Drugs Throughcare for Released Prisoners.* Research Findings 109. Home Office 2000.

Home Office (2001a): *Making Punishments Work: Report of a Review of the Sentencing Framework for England and Wales.* Home Office 2001.

Home Office (2001b): *Criminal Justice: The Way Ahead.* Stationery Office 2001.

House of Commons Employment Committee, *Employment in Prisons and for Ex-Offenders: minutes of evidence, Wednesday, 5 June 1991, National Association for the Care and Resettlement of Offenders.* HMSO 1991.

Joint Accreditation Panel (2000): *What Works: First Report from the Joint Prison/Probation Accreditation Panel.* HM Prison Service 2000.

Lyon, Juliet, and others, *Tell Them so They Listen: Messages from Young People in Custody.* Research Study 201. Home Office 2000.

Prime, Julian, *Criminal careers of those born between 1953 and 1978.* Statistical Bulletin 4. Home Office 2001.

Roberts, Marcus, *Young Adult Offenders: A Period of Transition.* Nacro 2001.

Simon, Frances, and Corbett, Claire, *An Evaluation of Prison Work and Training.* Occasional Paper. Home Office 1995.

Singleton, Nicola, *Psychiatric Morbidity among Prisoners in England and Wales.* Stationery Office 1998.

12 | Restorative Justice: An Exploration of Spirituality Within Criminal Justice

Tim Newell

L ENNY BURGLED MY HOUSE when I had been in the job for about a year. He apologized profusely when admitting to having broken into my rather sparsely furnished first bachelor home. In our discussion I was able to let him know how I felt about him going through my limited effects. But I will always remember that in an age when borstal training was based on personal development and a close attention to cleanliness and tidiness, backed up by regular inspections, Lenny's main message to me was that it was I who should really try to clean and tidy my home a bit more!

John was a life-sentenced prisoner in Grendon who had murdered. He attended a seminar with me on the subject of Forgiveness taken by the Bishop of Oxford, Richard Harries. John spoke about his feelings of inadequacy and his inability to come to terms with the idea of forgiveness. How can I ever be forgiven when I can never forgive myself? Six years later I met John, who is now a free man, after he had completed his therapy and had moved on from us. He said he was now able to accept what he had done and felt God's forgiveness as he began to rebuild his life in service to others.

Gary also was a life-sentenced man who had killed and kidnapped. Through therapy he came to an understanding of the effects of his actions on others' lives. He was devastated by his new realization and hated his actions more and more. He had tried to kill himself several times in other prisons but had been rescued by staff. He had completed five years in Grendon and it was time to move on to another prison. He could not face the prospect and decided that he wished to die with us. But he had so much respect for the staff and fellow prisoners in Grendon that he would not do it in a violent manner. He decided to die by not eating. He took out an advance directive against the prison through his solicitor that we should not intervene to feed him even when he lost consciousness. He began his fast that concluded with his death three and a half months later. He made his peace with his family and all who had had dealings with him in the prison. He expressed forgiveness for all of us – he did not want any of us to feel guilty or angry about his death. We should accept his death as a triumph over the past. Although a desperately sad time for many of us, there was a haunting dignity and humanity about Gary that will stay with me for all of my life.

It is these memories of relationships with people experiencing the pain of imprisonment – those whom we have locked away from our community – that have led me to consider the effectiveness of custody in enabling healing to take place. The limitations of working in prisons without understanding the context of the crime and the effect it had on the victims of the act have become more clear to me after working with those who realize what damage their behaviour has really had on others. Through this awareness I have listened closely to the voices of those affected by crime: the victim, the offender and to ourselves as members of communities.

The victim's voice has rarely been listened to in our development of justice systems. Lorraine's experience is telling. She visited a man in prison.

I felt a need to tell him the damage he had done – even if he hadn't have spoken to me – I still had this burning desire to strap him in a chair and just tell him everything that he had done. Not because he had killed my father, but how he had destroyed my family and continued to destroy my family – and that went on for ten years really – and the fact that my children grew up just knowing that my father had been shot as if it was a normal thing and I was quite angry that I had to explain to my son – that – well it happened and he's gone to prison and end of story. It just totally destroyed my family and it still has, 16 years later and there are still massive cracks that will never be repaired at all. I didn't feel bitter as in wanting to hurt him. I just wanted him to know what he'd done.

I asked the one main question. 'Do you regret killing my Dad?' And his answer was – 'The day your Dad died my life ended.' And it took me ages to work that out, to understand what that meant. At first I thought it was because he was so remorseful but it wasn't until the third visit that I realized that his life was over because he'd gone to prison, because he was caught.

And that's what I still have anger towards – that he hasn't accepted what he has done and taken responsibility for what he has done.

Lorraine needed the murderer of her father to know what he had done, she needed to find out if he felt remorse, she had to do this in person in order to move on in her own life. She continues to seek an understanding of remorse.

Viv's experience gives us another perspective on the innocent who are caught up in a crime. She is the mother of a young man who murdered a girlfriend. When he was arrested:

Life just stopped – it just worked around Andrew. Every day we went to prison to see him, while he was on remand. We went through the court trial with him. It was dreadful, people talking outside, they should hang him, they should do this, they should do that. I tried to keep my mouth shut and say nothing back in return although it was difficult.

There is nobody to help you. You've never faced that before. You don't know where you're going, you don't know what you're doing. It's just awful.

Your mind is just a total blank, it's complete shock. And people look at you as if you are a piece of dirt.

Until Andrew could admit what he had done, I was in denial as well with him. You know Andrew said, 'No I didn't do it.' Mum said, 'No he didn't.' But once he started to come to terms and I could see him starting to look a bit better in himself, then I could start to pick myself back up.

It broke my heart. I sat in a day here – it was a conference day I believe when we all met downstairs and Andrew said everything in front of everyone. And yes I suppose it came as a bit of a shock, but my words were, 'Well, look, I still love you. You're still my son. I still love you. And it's happened but we'll stand by each other.' And we have done.

Twenty-five per cent of all victims surveyed in the British Crime Survey said they wanted compensation from their offender, compared to only 9 per cent who wanted a prison sentence. Even among the group of victims who most wanted offenders locked up (burglary with entry victims), two thirds wanted non-prison sentences.

The offender told me of the struggle within prison to change and face the consequences. Tom is serving a long sentence for violent robberies.

> The crimes that I've been involved in were always about me getting and not about being aware of other people's feelings or the consequences of my actions on them – you know – how that would make them feel. And through looking at myself, with the help of other people, who went through the same kinds of experiences, might be different crimes but the same kind of emotions, to become aware of other people, and I've had to do that through the pain that I've suffered myself.
>
> Jail, like parents, has a huge responsibility in how it reacts to offenders, how it shapes offenders over a period of time, because you are talking about my 17-year sentence, I will do roughly 12 years out of that, and it can either shape me for the world, it can be either a barren place, like solitary, maximum security jails with the same sort of punishment attitudes where you don't feel that you've got a voice, where you don't feel anything less than a dangerous animal, or you can go along the lines of Grendon, where you can have an environment where it shows and shares trust, that it gives people something to live for, hope in themselves, by showing that there is a light side of somebody, and that is really encouraging that person, in what he might want.
>
> There are still days when I wake up, and I'm looking through the eyes of somebody who doesn't trust himself, who doesn't trust other people with my life, and that's from my early, early childhood, feelings of insecurity.
>
> So there are times when I wake up, and I feel comfortable in the dark in a sense, nobody can see me, I want to sit here, I want to lie here and think about my next big job and revel in the completion, the success of hitting a bank and stealing all the money and pissing everybody off, but it's much better in the light because people see that I can create something.

It is through the experience of such contacts and communications within relationships that I have begun to understand the need for another way to consider trying to manage the conflicts that arise from crime. Few sets of institutional arrangements created in the West have been such a failure as the criminal justice system. In theory it administers just, proportionate sentences that deter. In practice, it fails to correct or deter, just as often making things worse as better. Using John Braithwaite's theory of reintegrative shaming, it is quite clear why our justice system fails because it is primarily about stigmatizing, not about reintegrating. It is disrespectful, humiliating and often treats criminals as if they were evil people who have done evil acts. Reintegrative shaming means disapproving of the evil of the deed while treating the person as essentially good. Reintegrative shaming means showing a strong disapproval of the act but doing so in a way that is respecting of the person. The debate about the failure of the system has collapsed into a contest between those who want more of the same to make it work and those who advance the implausible position that it makes sense to stigmatize people first, and later subject them to rehabilitation programmes inside institutions. The debate has been between the justice model and the welfare model. See-sawing between retribution and rehabilitation has got us nowhere. If we are serious about improving the position we should look for a third model. That third model is restorative justice.

Tony Marshall's *Restorative Justice: an Overview*, published by the Home Office in 1999, gave us two definitions that are helpful in getting a sense of the approach to justice that challenges many assumptions of our current system:

- a problem-solving approach to crime which involves the parties themselves, and the community generally, in an active relationship with statutory agencies;
- a process whereby parties with a stake in a specific offence collectively resolve how to deal with the aftermath of the offence and its implications for the future.

Restorative justice is a set of principles in action:

- making room for the personal involvement of those mainly concerned (particularly the offender and the victim, but also their families and communities);
- seeing crime problems in their social context;
- a forward-looking (or preventative problem-solving orientation);
- flexibility of practice (creativity).

The objectives of restorative justice can be seen as:

- to attend fully to victims' needs – material, financial, emotional and social (including those personally close to the victim who may be similarly affected);
- to prevent re-offending by reintegrating offenders into the community;
- to enable offenders to assume active responsibility for their actions;
- to recreate a working community that supports the rehabilitation of offenders and victims and is active in preventing crime;
- to provide a means of avoiding escalation of legal justice and the associated costs and delays.

Restoring to victims a lost sense of empowerment is important as our processes often continue that disempowerment, giving the victim no say in the legal protocols. Restorative justice is about people deliberating over the consequences of a crime, how to deal with them and prevent their recurrence. It seeks to restore harmony based on a feeling that justice has been done. Finally, restorative justice aims to restore social support through involving loved ones in the consideration of events and their outcome.

Restoring to offenders dignity can have important components, facing up to the truth of the damage they have done. Restoring a sense of security and empowerment is often bound up with employment, and the involvement in discussing the consequences of crime adds to the educative nature of the process. To restore a sense of procedural justice to offenders is vital in achieving some legitimacy for the process.

Restoring community processes are contained in some of the rituals concerned with restorative justice, such as the support given to victims and offenders. Thus this justice is a bottom-up approach. Similar work can be carried out in school settings, neighbourhoods, ethnic communities, churches, through professions and so on, who can deploy restorative justice in their self-regulatory practices.

All cultures have deep-seated restorative traditions. Through observing the practice of restorative justice from countries where there has been more experience gained through the legacy of aboriginal spiritual and cultural community restoration, we can make connections with our own approaches.

The work of the Hollow Water Community Holistic Circle Healing (CHCH) in Manitoba, Canada, is the most mature healing process in justice integrating government-provided services (policing, justice, corrections, health and social services) within aboriginal culture and value systems. The benefits of the process of healing are often not reflected in research considerations, yet a recently published report from the Solicitor General's office in Canada and the Aboriginal Healing Foundation shows that as well as reducing reconviction rates, the process of restorative justice leads to improved well-being in communities. The cost-benefit analysis clearly demonstrates the effectiveness of implementing such a programme taking into account the financial, welfare and health benefits arising from such work.

The process is described in detail so that we can learn from what are not complex procedures but those that require a sense of valuing the participation of all involved and in trusting the underlying spiritual and communal healing forces to take effect. Hollow Water restorative practice is based on a 13-step process to handle conflict arising out of crime. The uniqueness of the victim, offender, families and workers' needs means that the process is continually evolving. As we explore the steps it might be worth considering where our own practice could match them.

Step 1 – Disclosure

Disclosures come from many sources, some accidental and some intentional. They could come from the victim, a family member, a spouse, someone from the community who witnessed an abuse, or even the offender. Members of the Resource Group are available for disclosure, and the person who received the disclosure has three responsibilities:

1 to get as much information as possible as to the facts of the allegation;

2   to continue as the 'natural' ally of the person who made the disclosure; and
3   to pass the information to the Assessment Team Co-ordinator immediately.

The Co-ordinator will then:

1   contact the police to inform them of the disclosure and to invite them to a meeting of the Assessment Team where the information will be discussed and a subsequent intervention planned;
2   call a meeting of the Assessment Team to discuss the disclosure, complete an assessment of the individuals and the families involved and plan the actual intervention that will follow. The plan will identify who is taking responsibility for what, and when. The safety of all family/community members will be a primary factor to be considered in planning the intervention;
3   ensure that all 13 steps of the process are followed in sequence (Steps 2 and 3 occur simultaneously)

Step 2 – Protecting the victim

The person from the Assessment Team taking responsibility for assisting the victim must:

• involve Social Services personnel;
• identify a safe home and make arrangements for the victim's stay;
• validate the disclosure, through an openness of process to start the beginning of a return to balance;
• take the victim to a safe home;
• ensure that an ally is available to the victim;
• ensure training and ongoing support to the safe home; and
• make whatever arrangements are necessary for the victim, for example a medical assessment or admission to a victims' group.

Step 3 – Confronting the offender

Although the protection of the victim takes priority, the main focus of dealing with abuse needs to shift to include the offender, dealing with the source of the problem and beginning the process of restoring balance within the individuals, families and community involved. The person taking responsibility for assisting the offender should feel comfortable with the alleged offender and see him/herself as a potential ally to the offender. This person must:

1 approach the alleged offender and confront him or her with the information gained in the disclosure;
2 explain that the victim has been removed and will be staying in a safe home until the community can resolve the situation (the other option, if the alleged offender is willing, would be to 'remove' the offender to a safe home);
3 explain that there is a good possibility (depending upon the severity of the offence, and his or her willingness to co-operate) that the matter could be handled by the community, in conjunction with the court system;
4 make it clear that any attempt at interference with either the process or the victim will result in the community assuming a secondary role and the matter being primarily handled by the court system;
5 ensure that an ally is available to the alleged offender; this ally will have to be very sensitive to the potential for suicide and/or violence towards others, and offer non-threatening and non-judgemental support, without reinforcing the alleged offender's denial system;
6 inform the alleged offender that it will be necessary for him or her to:
   • accept full responsibility for what has happened; and
   • undergo a psychological assessment if he or she is going to choose the community alternative;
7 tell the alleged offender that he or she will be contacted within five days as to:
   • what the community conclude after completing the assessment; and
   • what the community can offer in terms of dealing with the offence in a traditional healing manner;
8 make whatever arrangements are necessary for the offender, such as psychological assessment, admission to offenders' group, self-awareness course, and so on.

Step 4 – Assisting the spouse

As with the alleged offender, this can be a very difficult time for the spouse. Denial, anger, possible suicide and potential violence towards others are real possibilities. The person from the Assessment Team taking responsibility for the spouse must:

1 approach the spouse and present him or her with the information gained in the disclosure;
2 explain what has happened so far in terms of both the victim and the alleged offender;
3 explain the possibility of the matter being handled in the community, in conjunction with the court system;
4 ensure that an ally is available to the spouse; and
5 make whatever arrangements are necessary for the spouse, such as admission to a survivors' group, self-awareness course, women's therapy, and so on.

Step 5 – Assisting the family/community

In some cases the family of the victim and the alleged offender will be the same. In most cases they will be from the same community. In all cases the pain brought about by a disclosure will have a rippling effect throughout the community and many people will be affected.

The person from the Assessment Team taking responsibility for assisting families must:

1 approach appropriate members of the immediate family and present the information learned in the disclosure;
2 explain what has happened so far;
3 explain the possibility of the matter being handled by the community, in conjunction with the court system;
4 ensure that an ally is available for all members requiring this kind of support;
5 make whatever arrangements are necessary for the family members to join a survivors' group, women's therapy or self-awareness course, and so on.

Step 6 – Meeting of the assessment team, police and Crown Prosecutor

This meeting will be called by the Co-ordinator as soon (within four days of disclosure) as the first five steps of this process have been completed. The purpose of this is to:

1 present all information obtained so far;
2 decide how to proceed. There are three possibilities:
   - the facts do not support the allegation; in this case the victim would be returned to the family and the family worked with until it is back in balance;
   - the facts support the allegation, but for some reason (offence too serious, community response too limited, offender not willing, and so on) it is most appropriate for the court system to assume the primary role; or
   - the facts support the allegation and the offender should be given the chance of proceeding with the community alternative; in this case a Healing Contract would then be drawn up for presentation to the offender;
3 review responsibilities of respective meeting participants regarding the decision as to how to proceed (who will do what, and when).

Step 7 – Offender must admit and accept responsibility

The person from the Assessment Team taking responsibility for assisting the offender approaches the offender, and:

1 informs him or her of the outcome of the investigation;
2 explains the two primary alternatives available (community/legal; legal/community);
3. explain to the offender that, in order to restore his or her healing process, he or she must admit to the offence and accept full responsibility for his or her actions. To this end the offender must provide a voluntary statement (cautioned statement) to the police outlining his or her total involvement with the victim. This statement will be made with the full knowledge on the part of the offender that if:
4 the assessment team becomes aware of any victims

5 or information not included in the statement; and/or

6 the offender refuses to comply with the community alternative procedure at any point, and/or there is any recurrence of the offence the court system will immediately be asked to assume the primary role; and undergo a psychological assessment and agree to releasing the information obtained in this assessment to the Assessment Team;

7 present the Healing Contract; and

8 inform the offender that he or she has to:

- make a decision as to which primary alternative will be pursued; and
- inform the Assessment Team of this decision within two days. Failure to comply with the above would result in the court system assuming the primary role.

Step 8 – Preparation of the offender

If the offender admits to the allegations and is willing to accept the community alternative, he or she must then be prepared for the next step in the healing process: an appearance before a special gathering of the group, selected members of the family, the victim and selected members of his or her family. This preparation would be completed by the person from the Assessment Team who has taken responsibility for assisting the offender, and would include:

- an explanation of what will happen; and
- what will be expected of him or her.

Step 9 – Preparation of the victim

As with the offender, the victim must be prepared for the next step in the healing process, the appearance of the offender before him/herself, selected members of his or her family and the Group. The victim must be prepared to the point where he or she as at least willing to try to forgive the offender for what has happened. This preparation would be completed by the person from the Assessment Team who has taken responsibility for assisting the victim, and would include:

- an explanation of what will happen; and
- what will be expected of him/her.

Step 10 – Preparation of all the families

As with the offender and the victim, selected members of the families must be prepared for the next step in the healing process: the appearance of the offender before themselves, the victim and the Group. These members of the families must be prepared to be at least willing to try to forgive the offender for what happened. This presentation is carried out by the person from the Assessment Team who has taken responsibility for assisting the families and would include:

- an explanation of what will happen; and
- what will be expected of them.

Step 11 – The Special Gathering

Once the offender, the victim and selected family members have been prepared, the Co-ordinator will arrange for the offender to come face to face with:

1 the group of workers who represent the healing community;
2 the victim;
3 selected members of the family to answer for his or her misconduct.

The gathering will take place at a time and place agreed upon by all involved, and the seating arrangement will take the form of a circle.

The Special Gathering has ten steps:

1 The ceremonial opening. This marks the gathering as an event of importance. Preference about the exact nature of the opening will be given to the victim and offender but could include a song, a prayer, or some form of religious or traditional ceremony.
2 The Co-ordinator will address the gathering and explain its purpose as follows:
    - to hear details of the offence;
    - to speak publicly to the offender about the offence;

- to look at ways of dealing with the offence that will heal all persons involved and reunite the community;
- to demonstrate that such behaviour is unacceptable, but that healing is possible and supported;
- to learn something about sexual and violent abuse in general through an educational process, and
- to have all people present accept responsibility for supervising the Healing Contract.

3 The explanation of the offence. The Assessment Team members will then explain the offence.

4 The Co-ordinator then asks the offender if he or she:
- accepts the charges as true; and
- is willing to participate in the proceedings. If the offender rejects either or both conditions, the Co-ordinator explains that the gathering must be brought to a close and that the court system will be asked to assume the primary role. If the offender accepts both conditions, the gathering can continue. It is the community's responsibility to support the action of the Co-ordinator, based on the offender's decision.

5 The educational process. This part sets the stage for the rest of the proceedings and helps educate the people present about the seriousness and dynamics of the offence. It sets the emotional stage necessary for changes in attitude to occur. It is, in effect, a mini-workshop, and can include lectures, videos and handouts.

6 The offender verbally accepts full responsibility for his or her action. Now that all present have a better idea of what it is they are dealing with, the offender is asked to accept full responsibility for the offence, without rationalization, justification or reservation. Again, if the offender fully accepts the responsibility for the offence, the gathering can continue. If not, it is turned over to the court system as the primary agent. (If a break is necessary, this would be a good time. It will give people time to think about what they have learned, and to gather their thoughts about what they would like to say to the offender.)

7 The participants of the gathering speak. This is the heart of the traditional healing process, and allows the Community to show its concern for all involved. Here the people have a chance to speak openly to:

- the offender, telling him or her how they feel about the offence, encouraging him or her to accept full responsibility, and offering their support for his or her healing;
- the spouse, about his or her responsibility in helping the healing process, or perhaps talking to him or her about their part in the abusive situation if it is appropriate; and
- the victim, relieving him or her of any guilt he or she may feel, reassuring him or her that he or she is not responsible for the offence, and offering support.

When appropriate, and the offender, spouse and victim are willing, the idea of the family reuniting in the future (after the healing process has taken enough to ensure that such behaviour will not be repeated) is encouraged and supported. Members of the group are free, if they feel that it will help in the healing process, to relate their own experience in the past of being abused or being an abuser, and the problems that occurred as a result.

8 The Healing Contract is presented. At this point the Co-ordinator will present the Healing Contract developed in Step 6 to the whole group for their:

- comments and feedback;
- support;
- eventual supervision.

The Healing Contract addresses three general areas:

a. some degree of punishment, but the result must enhance the community as well as the offender's self-esteem. This would be likely to take the form of community service work;

b. protection against further victimization. This would be likely to take the form of restricted access to potential victims for a specified period of time;

c. treatment. This would be likely to take the form of individual counselling, attendance at support groups, and so on.

If the participants of the gathering, through consensus, recommend changes in the Healing Contract, the Co-ordinator will contact the police and the Crown Prosecutor before changing it.

9. The offender publicly apologizes and accepts the Healing Contract. At the request of the Co-ordinator the offender is now asked to:

- publicly apologize to:

- – the victim, accepting full responsibility for what has happened, and reassuring the victim that it will not happen again;
- – the spouse;
- – the group at large.
- publicly agree to abide by the conditions of the Healing Contract, and
- state that he or she understands that any failure to comply with the conditions will result immediately in the court system being asked to assume the primary role.

10. The Ceremonial Closure marks the gathering as an event of importance. Preference as to the actual content of the ceremony will be given to the victim and offender.

Step 12 – The Healing Contract is implemented

It is the responsibility of the Co-ordinator to ensure that the conditions of the Contract are implemented. The role of the participants of the Special Gathering in supervising the contract is essential to the healing of the offender, victim, their families and the community. Any failure of the offender to comply with the conditions of the Contract will result immediately in the court system being asked to assume the primary role.

Step 13 – The Cleansing Ceremony

This is a ceremony that marks the completion of the Healing Contract, the restoration to balance of the offender and a new beginning for all involved. The Co-ordinator will be responsible for arranging the ceremony at the appropriate time, which will depend upon the healing process for each individual offender. It is not anticipated that this will be before two years after the Special Gathering. The offender will have input into the ceremony, but it will be open to community and will be likely to include some form of a community feast. It is time to honour the offender for completing the healing contract and process.

13 | Christian Congregations and Criminal Justice

Julia Flack

THERE HAVE BEEN MANY WAYS in which Christian congregations have responded to criminal justice. Across time there are countless groups which have visited people in prison, and campaigned for changes in the system. The work of Quakers like Elizabeth Fry, and Free Church individuals such as John Howard, have been an inspiration to many reformers within criminal justice. Today there are groups from every denomination working at visiting prisons, and carrying out innovating work with offenders. One contemporary example is that of the Circles of Support in Canada, where released sex offenders have a group which supports them after release. This work is ecumenical, and has inspired an initiative in England from the Quakers to carry out similar work.

In these examples of faith-based involvement the work of the Church of England takes its place. There have been many reports on the criminal justice system, and debates in the General Synod, which is the central body of the church, where decisions can be taken about the future of the church. However, Synod also debates issues to do with national life. Among the topics debated in Synod there have been several discussions about prisons, the mandatory life sentence, and the work of the criminal justice system. This debate has been increasingly seen in an ecumenical context, where debates are set against the views of other churches, and even now other faiths. Clearly the question must be how far these debates resonate in the parishes. One of the persistent issues in the life of a body like General Synod, or any other denomination's central structures, is whether there is any impact on the day-to-day life of a parish church.

One way of answering that point is simply to describe one's own story and to say how this relationship worked out in practice. In 1985 I was elected to the General Synod as a representative of the Diocese of Wakefield. I quickly decided that my most effective contribution to the General Synod was to offer expertise and experience in a subject in which I felt confident. So, as a Probation Officer, my contribution would be in helping the General Synod in its work with criminal justice. I therefore made contact with the staff of the Board for Social Responsibility, and was later elected to the Board. This was a crucial time in the life of General Synod, for it was engaged in responding to *Faith in the City*.

This report was commissioned by the then Archbishop of Canterbury, Robert Runcie, and was very much his personal initiative. It was written by a group of experts, which included those with first-hand knowledge of living in deprived areas, and the report described the conditions in the large towns and cities in England. Poverty and deprivation were acute. The report was brought to Synod, and it represented a challenge to every congregation to respond to the issues of deprivation and injustice in England in the 1980s. The report was very controversial, and was attacked by the government.

There was a chapter on crime in urban areas, called 'Order and Law'. It talked a great deal about community responses to the problem of crime, and the need for better relations between the community and the criminal justice system. As a result of this report, Synod decided to respond to the challenge. A Synod penal affairs group, made up of magistrates, prison chaplains, probation officers, lawyers and prison visitors was set up to carry on this work in the area of criminal justice. There were discussions at each of the General Synod Sessions which not only involved those in criminal justice but also those involved in mental health, and in substance misuse. This of course reflected the complexity of the issue, as described in the chapter on crime in *Faith in the City*. That group still continues and has, over the years, examined a wide range of issues which have, in turn, fed into Synodical debates.

What was heartening from this discussion was that it was prepared to look at all issues pertaining to criminal justice and did not confine itself to prison affairs. That was extremely encouraging for those of us from other areas in the criminal justice system and enabled us to feel that we also had a part in the committee work of the General Synod. It also meant we were able to gain an insight into prison chaplaincy affairs that we would not have otherwise known.

In 1987 we began to examine how we could forward the dissemination of information into a wider forum than just the General Synod. As in many other areas of the church's life, it proved a difficult task to know exactly how to communicate the work that was being done by the Synod and its Boards into our dioceses, deaneries and parishes. We were spurred on by the then Chaplain General, the Venerable Keith Pound, who had recently asked each diocesan bishop to appoint a 'prisons link' person. Archdeacon Pound had been very troubled that the prison chaplains had seemed 'isolated' within their prisons and did not seem to be woven into any of the diocesan structures. This meant that they were relying totally upon prison and Home Office structures for their support. Our 'think tank' decided that we would use the link people and we would set up a series of diocesan groups which would not only examine issues of criminal justice but would also include the work of the prison chaplains. We were determined that these groups would be ecumenical and make every effort to include people from other churches. They were, additionally, a direct response to a recommendation in *Faith in the City* and a way of 'mainstreaming' that report into the structures of the dioceses. Diocesan and parish support for prison chaplaincy was a way of highlighting the issue of crime in the life of the church. We were committed to making sure that criminal justice was firmly on the agenda, not just of the General Synod, but of every diocese, deanery and parish. The question, which was uppermost in the mind of Synod was, 'How do we get this over to our parishes and the people in our pews?'

Underarching and supporting these groups were the biennial conferences that were set up in conjunction with the Chaplain of Lincoln Prison, Alan Duce. These conferences were both exciting and informative events. In my view they were also prophetic events. The formal inputs were led by people of considerable note in the field of criminal justice on both national and international levels. They were attended by people from both the voluntary and statutory sectors, many of whom held high office in their own organizations. (There is a description of them in the following chapter on the work of Bishop Bob Hardy.) Significantly, the conferences spanned an era when government policy was reacting to supposed public demand by becoming increasingly punitive. A massive prison-building programme was initiated because, in the government's view, 'nothing worked' in reducing crime except prison sentences.

Over the last 17 years there have been many changes in the life of the nation, and of the Synod. However, there have also been continuities as well. There continue to be diocesan groups, there have been General Synod debates, there have been day meetings in various dioceses on issues of criminal justice, there have been questions asked in the House of Lords, there has been a publication about sex offenders in the parishes, to name but a few of the initiatives. What is happening now is a fundamental review about the future of the Board for Social Responsibility. The Synod and its Committees have to look carefully at the future of their structures; it feels as if we are at a crossroads and need to ask, 'Should we continue this work?' and 'How can we continue this work?' Those two questions are what I shall address in this chapter.

I think we should continue this work and I hope passionately that we can. I look to a theological context to help understand why we continue. It seems to me that the field of criminal justice is totally relevant to my Christian faith. The Board for Social Responsibility has worked on the theology of criminal justice. It has published documents that have helped our thinking of the theological context of the work that is carried on at a day-to-day level. Simply put, the whole theme of crime and justice is woven into many of our biblical texts. I cannot forget, and indeed each Holy Week meditate on the fact, that the central act of our Christian faith, that of trial and crucifixion, informs the basic issues of crime and punishment with which I work.

I cannot, either, get away from the fact that whatever our religious persuasion or faith, we are members of community. Communities, like us all, are flawed organizations and inevitably there are people in those communities who commit offences and who do not comply with the norms and expectations of society. So, not only as Christians but also as citizens, we have to exercise a responsible and informed view of how society should, and can, function to be most effective and to provide the greatest good for the greatest number of people. It is my view that Christians should always have a view to the future – be 'prophetic' in relating to the issues of social justice. Promoting an involvement with restorative justice is beginning to be integrated into mainstream criminal justice practice. Championing restorative justice is prophetic work (Tim Newell writes about this issue in his chapter).

I think that if people in parishes and communities are informed about issues of criminal justice, they will discover that they have resources and talents which can help them to gain a fuller understanding and influence change by communicating to others.

So let me demonstrate my concern by drawing on my own experience in relating to the worlds of the criminal justice system and the life of the Church of England. This means working as a probation officer for 33 years. It also involves being a convenor of Criminal Justice Groups in two dioceses, a member of the General Synod Criminal Justice Group, and a member of the Board for Social Responsibility. I wish to suggest six models of continuing the work. I hope that these will be ways forward from the crossroads where I feel we now stand.

Model No. 1

Though it faces financial cutbacks, the Church of England has a very effective and efficient way of supporting the General Synod. This is through its Boards and Committees. The Board for Social Responsibility has a long and distinguished history in informing and being informed on a wide range of social issues. It is frequently asked to comment on new legislation and is also asked to participate in many forums of thinking and policy change. Similar bodies exist in the Roman Catholic Church, with the Bishops' Conference staff at Eccleston Square in London, and the Catholic Agency for Social Concern (CASC). CASC produced an influential report, *Women in Prison* in 1999, which is similar to the Board for Social Responsibility's 1999 report, *Prisons: A Study in Vulnerability.* Another example would be the Society of Friends, and their work on criminal justice. Tim Newell is a member of the Friends' national committee on criminal justice. Yet another is the 2002 report by the Methodist Church, *Young People in Prison,* or their 2000 report on rehabilitating sex offenders in the community.

In my view the work done by the staff of these bodies is crucial and necessary in maintaining the work of the churches in making sure that their response to issues of criminal justice is both effective and accountable. We cannot afford to do without it if we are to make a contribution to our communities. This indeed is the essence of the parish system of the Church of England, and of the national responsibility of the other denominations. I know that ecumenical co-operation within the various churches is a significant part of the work of Synod itself, and I know that people in the parishes can benefit from the work they do.

Model No. 2

Leaders of the churches are increasingly held in respect by other members and leaders of our communities. We should continue to develop the consultations that go on, covering a wide variety of subjects between the leaders of our communities and church members. I think it is important that on issues of criminal justice, the leaders in that field have opportunity to meet and discuss with leaders in the churches. This gives them the opportunity to discuss issues that are relevant to the communities in which everybody works. In the Diocese of Manchester many years ago, a former Director of Social Services used the structure of the Diocesan Board for Social Responsibility to set up a project for young juvenile offenders. The church funded this and it had the agreement of the Probation Service and the Social Services Department at executive level. It was perhaps the forerunner of the work now done by Youth Offending Teams in engaging the community in work with persistent young offenders. Such co-operation is not always easy to achieve because leaders of all aspects of our community have now got closely defined targets and areas on which their work must be focused. Nevertheless, the Crime and Disorder Act of 1998 set up community partnerships, and participation in the projects that have developed from these is one possible way in which the church can show its determination to participate fully in the lives of the communities in which we live in order to make them better and safer places. I do not advocate that all the work of the churches should be on a leadership level but, nevertheless, I consider that it is a necessary function to underpin local and parish work. The affirmation of our leaders gives the sanction and support of church and state and co-operation at its highest level.

Model No. 3

As I have suggested, one of the early points of action that we decided to promote were the diocesan groups. Not only did this come from the link persons that the bishops had set up in response to Archdeacon Pound but it emanated from recommendations made by *Faith in the City* in 1985. It was in that report that issues of conflict and inequality in the criminal justice system were first raised. These groups have largely progressed where there has been an enthusiastic group of people who have wanted to meet together, and share their practice and their experience of how their work or their voluntary work and their Christian faith had a meeting point. I have personally set up two of these groups and have given advice to many other dioceses setting them up.

There have been meetings of the members of these groups together in Church House, Westminster. They have been a very valuable part of the 'bread and butter work' of criminal justice in the dioceses and have been much appreciated by prison chaplains as a way of keying into diocesan structures and systems. Some dioceses have made specific efforts to enhance ecumenical membership, and this can be taken up by the new ecumenical body, Churches Criminal Justice Forum (CCJF), which is part of Churches Together in Britain and Ireland (CTBI). This body unites the denominations' work in criminal justice, and also works in the areas of education, interfaith dialogue, resettlement, family ties and volunteering. A good local example of ecumenical work would be the Devon Forum for Justice, which has existed for a number of years. The future surely lies in forming relationships with groups from other denominations, and even other faiths. In Blackburn there has been an interesting meeting of women from the Christian and Islamic communities on the issue of domestic violence.

Model No. 4: Parish involvement

This has been exceedingly difficult to develop because, as we all know, most congregations and faith communities have very heavy workloads in maintaining ministry. Attending to matters of social concern is not high on agendas, especially if they are trying to preserve buildings and be missionary organizations. However, the House of Bishops has statutory requirements for Child Protection Procedures that now have to be undertaken by each parish in respect of its volunteers and employees, and this has been a way of addressing social issues. People have had to learn insights about the protection of children and how their congregations need to be protected from targeting sex offenders. Recently, at a lay conference held by the Diocese of Ely, two workshops, led by a local prison chaplain, focused on the issue of child protection and the profile of sex offenders. The discussions were wide ranging and often painful, but it was a very interesting development and the group leader felt that people were beginning to grasp the issues which were so crucial for their understanding of the employment and deployment of volunteers and staff in the parish situation.

In the days of Alpha, Emmaus and other forms of lay ministerial training, I think it is crucial that criminal justice is included as part of our community and gospel imperative. The work of Alpha in Prisons links congregations and offenders. So too does the resettlement work carried out by the Churches Criminal Justice Forum, with two officers seconded from the Salvation Army. This helps congregations to be involved in resettlement. Another example is the befriending of sex offenders after release now being pioneered by the Society of Friends in England. The Home Office is piloting this model with the Society of Friends as the leading voluntary agency. The Circles model involves other churches as well at the local level. The first pilot in Guildford uses an Anglican parish congregation, while the Oxford one will involve Quaker groups.

Other examples are the Appropriate Adults scheme in Surrey, which is entirely run by the Church of England Diocese of Guildford, with volunteers drawn from many different churches. Appropriate adults accompany those under 16, and those with learning disabilities, in the criminal justice process, where a social worker cannot be present. Another use of volunteers from parishes is the mentoring schemes for young offenders now developed by churches in places as different as Swindon and Rochester.

Model No. 5: Prison chaplains

As I have indicated, the former Chaplain General, Keith Pound, was very exercised by the apparent isolation of many of the prison chaplains from diocesan structures. This is why he set up the 'prison links' persons with diocesan bishops. The whole issue of prison chaplaincy is now in a changing situation, and in another chapter of this book, the current Chaplain General, William Noblett, addresses those changes. But, taking all of those into consideration, prison chaplains still crucially need to be keyed into diocesan systems and local churches. In common with hospital chaplains, they frequently tell me how they value inclusion in diocesan and parish systems and how they benefit from being able to play a regular part in those systems.

I am fully aware of the fact that their funding and accountability is towards the Home Office. With sensitivity to the issues faced by prison chaplains, I think that there can be a symbiotic relationship developed with clergy in the community so that both can benefit from the exchange of information and working methods that are, at the same time common, but also very distinct. In his book *Prayers for People in Prison* William Noblett includes issues that affect both chaplains and congregations. It is a good model for our thinking. Events held in many areas in the annual 'Prisons' Week' in November have highlighted the advantages of sharing information.

Model No. 6: The use of volunteers

One of the ways in which the churches have been involved is calling together the many voluntary groups in prison. This work, initiated by Bishop Bob, has now been taken up by a group called CLINKS and by the Prison Service itself. The voluntary agencies cover a wide range of criminal justice related issues – the Prison Reform Trust, the Howard League, the substance misuse agencies, to name but a few. These agencies have had to struggle for recognition, to be accountable and to maintain financial viability. They have insights into issues of criminal justice that can be used in the education and prophetic work that the churches are called to achieve.

Similarly, the churches locally have always contributed towards the supply of prison visitors. Prison visitors are drawn from all parts of the community but are often managed by the chaplains and the chaplaincy in prisons. I have been very encouraged to know of Readers from the Church of England who have become prison visitors, thus viewing their ministry in a much wider context than serving the local church. The tightening up of security in the prisons has, of course, meant that the role of the prison visitor has changed but the networking role of chaplains, prison visitors and prison administration is often a tribute to the contribution of the local churches.

In the Church of England, the contribution of the Mothers' Union to many of the women's prisons over the last few years has been a growth area. Canon Jane Clay in her article mentions some of their work. Members now staff the visitors' centres, and provide clothing for mother and baby units. There are examples of Mothers' Union branches being set up at some of the women's prisons. In the Dioceses of Ely and Wakefield, the work done by the Mothers' Union in the prisons is a crucial part of the agenda of the Diocesan Mothers' Union. Similar work has been done by Roman Catholic agencies, such as the Union for Catholic Mothers (Helena Kennedy refers to their work on rape within marriage in her chapter).

Members of the Mothers' Union will recount how their staffing of Visitors Centres has led them on to further work with prison families which has been both affirming and reassuring to the families of people in prison. I do not advocate that 'church volunteers' necessarily need to break new ground or make policy, but the work of the Mothers' Union and prison visitors demonstrates that talent and service already exists in the parishes.

Is it all easy?

I would not wish to give the impression in my proposals that the incorporation of criminal justice is an easy part of mission. Realistically there are barriers to total effectiveness. First, not all practitioners and volunteers within the criminal justice system who are members of our congregations, Synods or other faith communities wish to make the link between their work and their faith and to develop their thinking and mission on that subject. This is not always understandable to the small band of people who are trying to promote a theological exploration of issues of criminal justice within their diocese, Synods or parishes.

Second, I have been made acutely aware on a number of occasions that some of the Models I have proposed can just be an excuse for a 'talk shop'. Most of us have pressurized lives and cannot afford to undertake work that does not have a definite outcome or is indeed 'value for money'. That is the reason, I would suggest, that the future of many of the diocesan groups has had to be reconsidered.

I therefore welcome the proposals that are coming from the Churches Criminal Justice Forum. Their grant from the Esmée Fairbairn Foundation is for two years. It enables a development worker (Stuart Dew) to focus particularly on restorative justice issues and promote this at a local level. I welcome this particularly because the wider community is looking towards that model both in its Crime and Disorder Partnerships and in particular in the work of the Youth Offending Teams.

During the last 20 years there have been significant shifts of government policy, and in our churches a broadening of the concept of ministry. I suggest that the following will be issues that emerge in the medium term:

- The work of the criminal justice and the faith communities must be as broadly based as possible. Without an interfaith/ecumenical perspective on criminal justice it is unlikely that we shall make any impact on injustices in the state system or, indeed, be able to offer it support. The work of the Churches Criminal Justice Forum is a great step forward.
- We cannot afford to be a 'talk shop' – we have to have identifiable outcomes for our activities that give parishes, deaneries, dioceses and other churches confidence that the time and effort they are putting in have some impact on the crime, punishment and criminal justice system, and help them to feel a part of it.
- The churches have both highlighted and investigated the restorative justice development as a means of achieving a fairer dispensation of justice. It has meant that restorative justice is now on the agenda of the denominations.

The picture inevitably is mixed. There has been great diversity in the way in which congregations have become involved in the criminal justice system. It is in the main an untold story. Recently the Home Office has become concerned to increase public participation in the criminal justice system, and to increase public confidence in its working. The story of church involvement in the last two decades is a story which deserves to be better known, for it is a means of enabling public participation to take place in many different ways. Churches are part of civil society, and in their work in the community, the networks of trust and support are strengthened. Congregations are part of that process, which enables the law to be held in respect by us all, and criminal justice to be about rehabilitation and not simply incarceration and retribution. In this work congregations do no more than follow the example of Jesus in Matthew 25.31–46 in caring for prisoners. The story of criminal justice groups in the churches over the last two decades is part of that story.

14 | Bishop Bob Hardy, Bishop to Prisons 1985–2001: A Tribute

Peter Sedgwick

THE MINISTRY OF BOB HARDY as Bishop to Prisons had an unusually wide scope. He came to this ministry in 1985, when David Faulkner, who contributes a chapter to this volume, was working on penal reform in the Home Office. Bishop Bob (as he became known everywhere) swiftly established his credentials by holding a series of conferences in Lincoln on criminology, which drew speakers from across the world. He also began to encourage the chaplaincy to see themselves as concerned with the life of the whole of the prison, ministering to prisoners, staff and indeed to volunteers and the wider community. He entered the House of Lords in 1993 and again established close working ties with penal reformers. In 1996 he added a third dimension to his ministry by chairing the Church of England's Board for Social Responsibility Home Affairs Committee. This committee covered the areas of criminal justice, substance misuse and mental health, and the Bishop attracted some notable experts to serve on the committee, some of whom contribute to this book. So, by the time of his retirement there was an inclusiveness about his ministry which was remarkable. He took part in many of the contentious debates on penal reform in the House of Lords. He visited chaplains, winning their trust as they faced the challenges of privatization of prisons and a steeply rising prison population. He also wrote and preached about the subject, chairing the launch of reports and working parties on the needs of prisoners, victims and all those caught up in the criminal justice system.

In many ways, he was the public face of the Church of England in penal matters, yet underneath this public role was a costly identification with the human issues of overworked chaplains, the families of prisoners, and prisoners themselves. When the system broke down, as in the riot at HMP Strangeways in Manchester, or the trial of prison officers for brutality at HMP Wormwood Scrubs, it moved him deeply. He was present when chaplains, sometimes senior ones, found they could no longer carry on from exhaustion and strain, and his ministry was there being alongside them.

However, it was not simply a mission of compassion and identification. There were enemies to be confronted as well. These could be in the shape of public opinion, with its punitive and stereotyped view of sex offenders, which he challenged sharply both through public comments, and the publication of *Meeting the Challenge*.[1] The purpose of the report was to ask how sex offenders on release from custody, and under the strictest supervision, could be re-integrated into congregations. Many sex offenders are deeply religious, and a congregation can offer both a place to worship and a community to support their needs. However such care can be exploited as well. The report, written for the Home Affairs Committee by Mrs Julia Flack, who also writes in this book, did not have an easy reception in the church. There was much anxiety about its reception, and attempts to prevent its publication. However, the report sold 6,000 copies in a few months, and was widely taken up by the Probation Service across England. It was followed by a larger report from the Methodist Church and the setting up of a friendship scheme for sex offenders by the Society of Friends. The Anglican report paved the way for this work.

Other enemies were there in the shape of politicians, who played to the public appetite for harsh punishments and longer sentences. Yet in public the dialogue remained courteous, if firm: this was a prophetic ministry, but one conducted through a dialogue with ministers and the press. In private his views were very clear about the behaviour of some politicians.

Such a ministry suggests that it is still possible for there to be a Christian input into the future of criminal justice in England. This is not an imperialist contribution, which ignores the work of other faiths: one of his final acts as the Home Affairs Committee met for the last time was to invite the Muslim adviser to prisons, who had addressed the committee on the need for an interfaith perspective on prison chaplaincy, to close the meeting with an Islamic prayer. It was a gracious gesture, affirming how deep the links are between the Abrahamic faiths of Islam, Christianity and Judaism. Yet at the same time he was resolute in defending the integrity of Christian chapels against moves by the Prison Service to make them dual-use for recreation, or other purposes.

In this tribute, I will highlight a number of aspects of this wide, and yet coherent ministry. Chaplaincy is the first area to be addressed. Then we move to the Lincoln conferences, and so on to his public role in the Lords, along with the moves for penal reform, which he supported. Finally, there are the many other aspects of his work with voluntary groups, the Home Affairs Committee, and much else, which can only be mentioned in passing. He has left this ministry at a time when the Prison Service is undergoing even greater changes, as it faces up to the implications in the review of sentencing carried out for the Home Office by John Halliday in 2001. Prison chaplaincy is also changing fast, as the recognition of a ministry shared by all the major world faiths becomes more pronounced. What remains of lasting value in his ministry was that he held prisoners and offenders before the church and the wider public, so that they were not forgotten. Perhaps his greatest achievement was to show that faith communities were not to be relegated to a private sphere of personal opinion, where religion becomes a leisure pursuit as though it were some esoteric hobby. He left both the chaplaincy and the views of faith communities respected by both the Prison Service and the Home Office.

This is a major contribution, which, as David Faulkner shows in his chapter, can help to balance the stress in public services on efficiency and management. This, while no doubt very necessary, can easily lose sight of the overall values, which the organization serves. Christianity, like the other faiths, must always acknowledge these goals, but it can also question their tendency to marginalize the human needs of those who spend their days inside the criminal justice system. Prisons need to be run as cheaply as possible, and not to waste public money, but Sir David Ramsbotham shows in his chapter that there is much more to their work than cost savings. Sometimes, in the late 1990s, it seemed as if the General and the Bishop were forever in the news, supporting the work of reform groups such as the Prison Reform Trust, the Howard League, and many others. It was through such publicity, underpinned by scores of visits to prison establishments, that prison reform is slowly and painfully carried forward.

Chaplaincy

The brief for the post of Bishop to Prisons did not exist when Bishop Bob took over in 1995. (He sometimes told the story that Archbishop Runcie said that he wanted a bit of a thug to be Bishop to Prisons. While this amused him, he also said that this was a profound misunderstanding of the role from a man he deeply admired.) On his retirement he spelled out the job description for his successor, Peter Selby, Bishop of Worcester, and it is worth quoting the document in full:

> When I was appointed Bishop to HM Prisons there was no job description and really no documentation. Eventually a Licence from the Archbishops of Canterbury, York and Wales was produced to enable me to move freely across diocesan and provincial boundaries, and the Home Office gave me a Prison Service Security pass.
>
> I have tried to develop the job along three particular lines:
> 1   To be a resource and support to the Chaplain General and the Prison Service chaplaincy through:
>   – the Ecumenical Chaplaincy Group (meeting with other church leaders)
>   – the Prison Chaplaincy Advisory Group (meeting three times a year with the Chaplain General, Chaplains in this field, a magistrate, a prison governor and a representative of Prison Fellowship)
>   – attendance at all the Chaplaincy assessment centres (for the selection of prison chaplains).
> 2   To be a bridge between the prison world and its ministry, and the regular life of the Church of England, through:
>   – the General Synod Penal Affairs Group (which I organise during each Synod)
>   – supporting the network of Order and Law and Criminal Justice Groups across the Dioceses of the Church of England
>   – keeping criminal justice issues before the church and helping other bishops in their concerns with prison ministry.

3 To be an advocate for Christian values and concerns within
   the criminal justice system through:
   – being familiar with the prison system (visiting individual
     establishments)
   – speaking on criminal justice matters in the House of Lords
     and elsewhere
   – developing links with the other agencies working within
     the criminal justice systems, especially those concerned
     with its reform and improvement.
   – being prepared to take up individual cases where there is
     thought to be neglect or injustice.

Two comments are worth making on this document. First, the Bishop
spent much of Advent travelling round prisons listening to chaplains,
and he also devoted much time to interviewing prospective chaplains.
This meant that he got to know chaplains well, and his ministry became
a personal one to many who had been appointed by him. The formal
lines of accountability to the local prison governor, and to the Chaplain
General through various levels of management, remained in place.
However, Bishop Bob provided an informal and discreet additional
support, which enabled chaplains to consult him about their work, and
about their move on to other posts after they left the Prison Service.
The Bishop also supported the Chaplain General in his dealings with
the Home Office and Prison Service. There were many difficult issues
to deal with, such as privatization of prisons (who appoints the chaplains, assuming that they existed at all?) and the need for cost savings.
Increasingly the multi-faith issue became the most important one, in
which the Bishop maintained good relationships with other faiths,
while defending the existence of a Christian chaplaincy, and not merely
'religious provision' run by a civil servant. It was a source of pleasure
that governors in prisons appointed additional assistant chaplains, and
that the Chief Inspector's reports praised the chaplaincy.

The second comment draws on Bishop Bob's own reflections on this
ministry. He preached about it on several occasions, and one of his
sermons appeared in *Crucible*.[2] He also wrote about it in the BSR report
Prisons: A Study in Vulnerability[3] and commended chaplaincy in the
General Synod debate.

In his sermon given in 1997 in Great St Mary's Church, Cambridge, he spoke of chaplains as amphibia. Like frogs, they move between dry land and water. Caught up in the criminal justice system, they are constrained by the harsh realities of life: lack of resources, the anger of prisoners, and the frustration of prison officers. But the theological role of a chaplain is where they swim freely, handling guilt, anger, forgiveness and hope through their theological reflections. Theology is a way of coming to terms with the depraved and sinful nature of life: 'In a theological view chaos is always on the edge of things.' Prison is no different, and theology enables the chaplain to respond with dignity and hope to the chaos in people's lives. In a searching examination of the issues, the sermon moves over the need to preserve the worth of prisoners, the importance of relationships, the irreducible nature of justice, and finally about forgiveness. He spoke at length on restorative justice and its potential for use in the prison system (Tim Newell's chapter expands on this).

The article in the prisons report was co-authored with the Chaplain General. This is a striking article, drawing attention to the noise and constant movement in prisons, their opportunities for bullies and the authoritarian to intimidate the weak, and the vast well of loneliness and hurt that is there. Chaplains have to be able to handle themselves with self-knowledge and a firm grasp of what they are trying to do. Prisoners are honest, direct, spontaneous and humorous, and a chaplain must be alert to the opportunities which prison life offers. Much of this description could be applied to the Bishop himself: apparently letting a story unfold, but in fact weighing up carefully with great shrewdness the right way to intervene, and blending this intervention with humour, directness and a down-to-earth approach. Anecdotes about the Bishop are legion, all of them tinged with humour, respect and affection. The least pompous of men, he could carry an innate personal dignity into any situation or act of worship. He also carried an enormous understanding of prisons, which drew on years of experience, visits, conversations and researching the subject.

The Lincoln Conferences

The Bishop put a great deal of energy into these four conferences, which were arranged by the chaplain at Lincoln Prison, the Revd Alan Duce. They attracted a huge number of people from across the world.

They lasted from 1989 to 1995, and were held every two years for three days in July. The attendance was around 250, and they were chaired by the then Chief Inspector of Prisons, Sir Stephen Tumim, who was a former judge. His conviviality added to the friendliness of the occasion. Each conference had a theme. These were, 'The Meaning of Imprisonment' (1989); 'Respect in Prison' (1991); 'Relationships in Prison' (1993); and 'Peace in Prison' (1995). Speakers in 1989 included Nils Christie from Oslo; Norval Morris from Chicago; and the then Bishop of Durham, David Jenkins. In 1991 Howard Zehr, the world authority on restorative justice, came from the United States, and debated with Lord Quinton. The third conference had Elisabeth Kübler-Ross, who was another internationally famous psychiatrist, Duncan Forrester, and a Norwegian criminologist. The final conference had the Archbishop of Canterbury and Diana Lamplugh, the mother of Susie Lamplugh, speaking on peace in prisons.

The political climate in the 1990s had swung far away from the reforming programme, which had been present in the Home Office in the previous decade. Many people were filled with despair about the soaring prison population and the punitive rhetoric of politicians. These conferences filled an important national role, opening up the criminal justice world to a wider audience. They were to prove as well a preparation for Bishop Bob's role in the Lords, and as a penal reformer.

Debates in the House of Lords

In an article in the *Church Times* on 19 November 1999, the Bishop reflected on the work of the House of Lords. The occasion was the passing of the majority of the hereditary peers, as a first stage of the reform of the Lords. He spoke of the frustration of managing his own diary, when parliamentary debates could occur at short notice. Often there was only a fortnight's notice, or less, and that had to be balanced with commitments to the diocese. Sometimes he would stay as late as he could, but then catch a train back to Lincoln, arriving after midnight for the next day's work in the diocese. Nevertheless there was a strong contribution to be made, both representing Lincolnshire as the Bishop of Lincoln, and speaking about the issue of prisons. There were speeches across the years on schools, transport and spending assessments, which all affected the county of Lincolnshire.

In his article he argued that the second chamber could scrutinize the legislation put forward by the government, which was often pretty badly drafted. The House of Lords was both independent, and contained many peers who had great expertise. He quoted John Stuart Mill, 'Truth emerges from the clash of adverse opinions.' Bishops could provide a spiritual perspective, which drew on Christian values and teachings. 'Our role as chaplains to the House should not be forgotten nor underplayed.' There was a strong sense of regret in Bishop Bob's eulogy for the contribution made by hereditary peers in the Lords over the centuries. He supported Lord Strathclyde's opinion that peers could give a sense of 'what counts in the long term rather than the passing fashion of the hour'.

It was not then as someone who wanted to challenge the Prison Service because he was opposed to authority that Bishop Bob spoke often in the Lords. Instead his vision of social and political order was more organic, drawing on the wisdom of experience and of tradition, which was embedded in institutions such as the House of Lords. He spoke of the reform of the Lords as creating 'restless and uncomfortable days', which could continue for some time to come, until the new constitutional order (whatever it was) stabilized. However, he was also aware that much needed to be said about the conditions in prisons, even in this uncertain time, when the government had a tendency to write off debates in the Lords.

He took his seat in the Lords as Bishop of Lincoln on 2 February 1993, introduced by the Bishops of London and St Albans, and remained there until his retirement in the autumn of 2001. His maiden speech on 12 January 1994 (which, by convention, was not controversial) was in a debate on pornography and violence in broadcasting. He referred to young offenders in his speech, mentioning how many inmates at a Young Offenders' Institution were watching horror videos when he visited the establishment.

Bishop Bob contributed to many prison debates in the Lords during his eight years as a peer, beginning with a debate on 2 February 1994 on prison overcrowding. It was a theme he would return to many times in the next few years. Local prisons, such as Lincoln, were overcrowded because of the increase in remands to custody. Offending on bail and offending by young people had led to a large number of young people being moved 'far from their families, with the result that anxiety and tension increase'. The Bishop drew, as he often did, on his personal experience of visiting prisons, 'Many prisoners are much more interested in such issues as getting units of freedom, more telephone calls, better visits, more home leave and custody nearer home.' Slopping out was an evil, but these were issues which really mattered. Above all, the problem was that the deepest questions were ignored:

> These are to do with the way that the government have rapidly increased the public impression that punishment will in the short term ease long-term social problems. The problem is compounded by disillusion among prison staff about the usefulness of their work and its security, as they see more and more violent and dangerous people sent to prison to be held in more relaxed circumstances.

This speech combined many of his concerns. There was certainly the problem of sanitation and overcrowding, but behind this were three far greater difficulties. One was the political agenda of imprisoning more and more people. Second, there were the feelings of prisoners themselves, and their contact with their families. Third, there was the morale of staff, which was always central to his thinking. He never failed to see the job of being a prison officer and governor as a very high vocation, whatever the difficulties of exercising that role, and whatever his views on individual members of staff.

In May 1994 he challenged the government's plan to curtail the rights of the suspect and defendant on arrest during the Criminal Justice and Public Order Bill. The tradition of a silent and innocent defence lay deep in scripture, where Isaiah was 'oppressed and he was afflicted and yet he opened not his mouth'. The same words are applied to the suffering of Jesus in Acts 8, where Philip baptizes the Ethiopian eunuch. 'That tradition gives the Christian Church a special concern for the rights of the innocent and particularly those who are weak and not readily able to speak for themselves.' It was typical of Bishop Bob that he wove together this argument with the findings of the recent Royal Commission on Criminal Justice and the legal tradition in England. Once again we see a deeply organic view of custom, scripture and law protecting the rights of the innocent. 'Drawing adverse inferences from the silence of suspects and defendants on arrest in the police station and during trial would, in the opinion of many it seems, reverse the traditional presumption of innocence.'

The next few years saw many such interventions. In December 1996 he challenged another government plan to extend the use of criminal conviction certificates, pointing out that this plan could undermine the successful re-integration of offenders into society. As ever, he turned back to Christian theology and tradition, citing the recent lecture by the Archbishop of Canterbury to the Prison Reform Trust. He quoted the Archbishop, 'restoring relationships requires positive attention to the relationships by which the offender can be restored and rehabilitated and helped to avoid the temptation of further crimes'. In February 1997 he challenged the Prison Service on the difficulties caused by ever-changing release dates for those who were arranging accommodation and job schemes.

In June 1997 he spoke at length on prison education, in a debate initiated by Lord Longford. This was one of several 'Longford debates' he was to participate in during his time in the Lords. Even though there was now a Labour government, there were great cuts in prison budgets, adding up to 5 per cent a year for three years. The soft targets for cuts were always education and resettlement. As so often, he paid tribute to the prison staff, pointing to training programmes to do with reducing re-offending, drug treatment and sex offender programmes, and training workshops. 'The work ethic is important in the prison world.' Cuts would put all this at risk, demoralizing staff and making prisoners sceptical of resettlement programmes. In a familiar note he recognized that efficiency savings had their place, but said that such savings were jeopardizing the stability and calm of prisons. Prisoners were being moved around, as numbers grew and budgets were reduced. All that would happen would be the release of embittered prisoners, who had not come to terms with their offences or who they were. 'The real hope in the Prison Service is to build upon the dedication and commitment of prison staff, particularly those in education and probation who are working effectively with prisoners.' In December 1997 he asked the government to confirm that it was its wish to stop remanding 15- and 16-year-olds into custody.

In October 1998 he sponsored the only debate in his name during his period in the Lords. Christopher Edwards was killed tragically in Chelmsford Prison in November 1994 by a fellow inmate. The inquiry into his death reported in June 1998, and the matter was taken up in the House of Commons. His parents, Paul and Audrey, appealed to the European Court of Human Rights about the death and the subsequent inquiry. The Bishop arranged a debate in the Lords to draw attention to the plight of mentally disordered offenders. Paul and Audrey Edwards sat with me in the gallery of the Lords as they heard the Bishop refer to Christopher's death, and call on the government to ensure that such events never happened again. He mentioned the review of the Mental Health Act, which the government had set up, and the need to improve court diversion schemes for the mentally ill. While the debate had to await the result of the appeal to the European Court on the Inquiry, and no formal apology was made (for legal reasons), nevertheless a government minister expressed his deepest regret at what had happened in the debate. Paul Boateng, MP, the minister for mental health at the time, listened to the debate at the bar of the House as well. It was some sort of satisfaction for the Edwards, and the condition of mental health services in prison was properly exposed. In March 2002 the European Court found that Christopher's death breached Article 2 of the Convention on Human Rights, on the right to life, and that his parents had been denied the right to participate in the inquiry. It condemned both the Prison Service and Essex police. Today the Prison Service and the NHS are working together to improve mental health in prisons. Paul and Audrey Edwards are members of their local congregation in Essex and continue to campaign for restorative justice. Here was an example of where a Lords debate could speak to a tragic event, and yet try to bring good out of evil.

Three final debates in the Lords should be mentioned. In February 2000 there was a debate on the highly critical report by Sir David Ramsbotham on HMP Wandsworth after an unannounced visit by Sir David as Chief Inspector to Prisons in July 1999. The Bishops of Lincoln and Southwark both spoke, with the Bishop of Southwark paying an equally unannounced visit to the prison the night before the debate to see conditions for himself, much to the amazement of the prison staff. Once again Bishop Bob mentioned the issue of mental health, referring to 'filthy conditions and idleness' in the health care wing. Prison staff were being asked to deal with the mentally ill in ways that were beyond their capabilities, although that did not excuse their failures. Staff morale was low, and the culture of the prison was poor. He also expressed a great deal of concern at the ability of prisoners to get to chapel, saying that this was a right and not a recreation. Once again he emphasized the positive aspect, looking to the new governor to provide a way out of the troubles of the prison.

Second, during the contentious attempts by the Home Secretary in 2000 to limit the role of the Chief Inspector of Prisons by amalgamating the post with the Chief Inspector of Probation, he expressed strong opposition to the plan, both in the Lords in October 2000 and in submissions to the Home Secretary. The plan was dropped, and Anne Owers is now a distinguished successor to Sir David. Equally he opposed the attempts to make benefit conditional on attendance at meetings with probation officers for offenders under supervision. He supported and moved amendments with Lord Windlesham and Baroness Kennedy. In a speech on 17 April 2000 he set out his case. This punishment was in effect double punishment, adding withdrawal of benefit to whatever fines or imprisonment were imposed by the courts for breaching a probation order.

> Benefits are, understandably, set at subsistence level. Many probation officers working with offenders would not find it acceptable morally to push them and their families into further debt and destitution. In making the probation officer responsible for sending the appropriate certificate to the benefits office, the legislation undermines and destroys any trust that has been built up between the probation officer and the offender. I should like to remind the House that trust is all-important if effective care and rehabilitation is to take place.

The amendment was successful, though a pilot scheme remains in place.

The final debate to mention was his last speech, on 11 July 2001, in a debate initiated by Lord Hurd, chair of the Prison Reform Trust and former Home Secretary. This debate also saw the last speech made by Lord Longford before he died: it was somehow appropriate that the two men were together in the Lords on the subject of penal reform, for which they had both fought so hard. The Bishop took up once more the issue of mental illness in prisons, welcoming the advances made, but pointing out that many prison doctors did not even hold a GP qualification. Facilities were still poor, even if there were splendid examples of voluntary sector provision such as the First Night in Custody scheme in Holloway (Myra Fulford writes about this in this book). There were also 86 per cent more children in prison in 1999 than in 1993. He referred to the campaign by the Children's Society to get children out of prison. He ended by appealing to the new Home Secretary to take some risks. Christian ministry was about the vulnerability of love, and that involved risk-taking, which broke new ground. If the Home Secretary would respond in this way, it would offer 'real hope to those of us who care about our prisons'. It was a very characteristic way to end his ministry in the Lords. He challenged governments, of whatever party, not to ignore prison life. The evils of prison life were set out starkly, yet he was as ever prepared to co-operate with measures to improve the situation, and he recognized the new signs of a more compassionate regime. All this was grounded in an appeal to theology set alongside the results of his research.

Other commitments

Much could be said of Bishop Bob's many other commitments, but they can only be mentioned briefly here. For many years he convened the voluntary organizations in prison, and spoke on their behalf in the Lords. CLINKS and the Prison Service are now undertaking this co-ordination. He also supported the diocesan criminal justice groups, and the Penal Affairs group at General Synod. In the Home Affairs Committee, he chaired meetings on deaths in custody, personality disorder, racism in the criminal justice system (including a moving meeting with Neville Lawrence), and especially the issue of women in prison. All this meant many hours of preparation, shaping the draft of reports, and meeting with conference participants. It was his contribution to a fairer prison system.

Conclusion

It is difficult to capture the essence of the man behind the list of chaplaincy visits, conferences, speeches and writings. What was central was that he sought to be quite a traditional bishop, who saw with great clarity that his own diocese needed to innovate in new patterns of ordained ministry, and that prison chaplaincy likewise could not ignore the realities of a multi-faith society. He did not seek controversy for its own sake. Rather his deep love for the vulnerable, his understanding that his priesthood gave him the language to confront evil, chaos and violence in human beings without being either sentimental or condemnatory about their past actions; his ability to convey his presence with the force of his personality, while remaining humorous and down to earth; his enormous reliance on prayer coupled with his friendship with people interested in criminal justice of all religions and none: all these made his ministry as Bishop to Prisons over 16 years one that will be remembered with gratitude and admiration.

(I am grateful to Alan Duce and Raymond Rodger for help with the background to this chapter.)

Notes

1   Flack, Julia, *Meeting the Challenge: How Churches Should Respond to Sex Offenders*. Church of England Board for Social Responsibility Home Affairs Committee, 1999. Download from:
    <http://www.cofe.anglican.org/view/meeting_the_challenge.rtf>.
2   'Changing Lenses: Theology and Criminal Justice', *Crucible*, October 1998.
3   Published by Church House Publishing, November 1999. The text of past and present debates in the House of Lords is at:
    <http://www.parliament.the-stationery-office.co.uk/pa/ld/ldhome.htm>.

Index